The Ideology of Progress, World Culture, and Animal Protection

Lora Stone

UNIVERSITY PRESS OF AMERICA, ® INC.
Lanham • Boulder • New York • Toronto • Oxford

Copyright © 2007 by
University Press of America,® Inc.
4501 Forbes Boulevard
Suite 200
Lanham, Maryland 20706
UPA Acquisitions Department (301) 459-3366

Estover Road
Plymouth PL6 7PY
United Kingdom

Library of Congress Control Number: 2006933921
ISBN-13: 978-0-7618-3608-7 (paperback : alk. paper)
ISBN-10: 0-7618-3608-X (paperback : alk. paper)

Contents

Introduction

During the twentieth century, many industrialized countries experienced both an increase in meat consumption and the emergence of organizations dedicated to animal protection. Although theories of modernization and world-systems can explain the increase in meat consumption that often accompanies economic expansion, they do not address how and why animal protectionist groups and critiques of meat consumption emerge with this same economic expansion . Since these protectionist groups and critiques are not bound strictly by national borders and national culture, questions related to both increased meat consumption and emergent protectionist norms should involve an examination of world-level culture for possible answers.

Based on examination of 1) the changing status of non-human animals, 2) increased meat consumption, 3) the role of the nation-state in animal protection, and 4) the emergence of non-governmental organizations dedicated to animal advocacy and protection, this book emphasizes that both animal protection and increased meat consumption occur with the expansion of a world-level culture and its ideology of progress. This world culture defines animal protection, including the alleviation of pain and suffering, as a necessary value and goal of the progressive, ideal nation-state and its citizens. This same world culture has defined meat consumption, perceived as nutritionally necessary and indicative of socio-economic development, as a definitive characteristic of the progressive, ideal nation-state.

Clearly promoted and institutionalized during the twentieth century, both animal protection and meat consumption were ideologically defined much earlier as characteristics of a *progressive* society. Although developed initially in transnational epistemic communities as early as the eighteenth century, this ideology of progress is now an essential element of a world-level culture that prompts individual and corporate actors to react according to universalistic

1

models of rights and justice predicated on assumptions regarding social progress. Given that the global, concurrent rise of meat consumption and of organized animal protection are both grounded in a shared ideology of progress, this book examines both phenomena, as well as the rise of related legislation by nation-states and the increasingly important role of non-governmental organizations. The puzzle yet to be solved involves the global patterns of increased meat consumption and of increased animal protection, all supported in part by an ideology of progress, converging with an exponentially increasing global human population that is confined to a finite amount of natural resources. During the latter decades of the twentieth century, global protectionist norms that address this problem emerged and began influencing individual and corporate behavior. True solutions, however, involve globally redefining ideas of progress and how they inform action and policy at all societal levels.

In Chapter 1, "Population, Consumption, and Protection," context for the book is provided in an examination of the relationships between population and food production, changing patterns of food production, distribution, and consumption, and the emergence and growth of organized animal protection and animal rights.

Chapter 2, "Animal Protection and the Ideology of Progress," is a historical analysis of the principles and ideologies presented by animal advocates, beginning with the ideology of progress emerging from epistemic communities in the late eighteenth century. Following the explanation of the origins of the ideology of progress and its relation to the changing status of non-human animals, the remainder of the chapter covers the beginnings of formal animal protection in the nineteenth century and its subsequent development. Animal protection is shown to be a characteristic of the ideal nation-state, as defined first in an ideology of progress, and later as a value and goal of world culture. Political, social, and cultural context are discussed, with representative statements included in the chapter.

Chapter 3, "Increased Meat Consumption and the Ideology of Progress," includes a longitudinal analysis of quantitative data from United Nations databases, as well as economic, social, and cultural quantitative and qualitative data related to meat consumption in selected countries. Collection and reporting of data for many developed countries has been consistent and reliable since 1960, thus much of this chapter will focus on patterns and trends that are evident beginning around 1960. Although estimations of meat consumption previous to 1960 will be discussed, these estimations will provide rich historical context and general comparisons, rather than statistical certainty. As with animal protection, meat consumption is shown to be a characteristic of the ideal nation-state, as defined first in an ideology of progress, and later as a value and goal of world culture.

Chapter 4, "Animal Protection and the Nation-State," discusses historical and ideological changes in the regulation of animals as food. This chapter is a qualitative examination of the regulation of the use of animals for human consumption, beginning with an historical overview of the religious regulation of killing and using animals for food purposes. This overview is then followed by a discussion of changes occurring with the rise in state authority over religious authority, and the related rise of animal protection. The increased role of the nation-state is shown to be a consequence of the expansion of world culture and the ideology of progress, with then nation-state described as being part of a nexus that disperses elements of world culture.

Chapter 5, "Animal Protection and Non-Governmental Organizations," identifies, describes, and analyzes NGOs that include animal protection in their mandates, being in some manner dedicated to animal advocacy and protection. This chapter includes a comparative overview of the definitions and functions of NGOs, and an analysis of the role of NGOs in the advancement of animal protection. The overview of NGOs provides an important foundational understanding of how culture is used to define animal protection as a necessary characteristic of societies and their governments, as well as direct individual and corporate actions into appropriate social change related to animal protection. As with nation-states, NGOs are described as being part of nexus that disperses elements of world culture.

The final chapter, Chapter 6, "World Culture and Animal Protection," presents conclusions drawn from the examinations and analyses in the previous chapters, including the assertion that concurrent shifts in the status of non-human animals and in levels of global meat consumption were grounded in an ideology of progress that promoted both animal protection and improved nutrition for all citizens. Another important conclusion is that this ideology of progress is a fundamental element of contemporary world-level culture, and is conveyed through a nexus that includes nation-states and NGOs. Through this nexus, animal protection is asserted as both a value and a goal of world-level culture, with both the ideal society and its individual citizens expected to manifest these values and goals. Finally, while the book as a whole examines but one cluster of related phenomena involving ideas of progress, the human consumption of animals as well as the protection of animals, and related elements of world-level culture and society, it also directs much needed attention to human population growth and to patterns of food production, distribution, and consumption, all of which have becoming increasingly critical issues.

Chapter One

Population, Consumption, and Protection

During the twentieth century, many industrialized countries experienced both an increase in meat consumption and the emergence of organizations dedicated to animal protection. This book explores the history and examines the data directly related to this concurrent increase in meat consumption and animal protection. In a broad sense, this work is the result of a growing interest in three areas: the relationship between population and food production; changing patterns of food production, distribution, and consumption; and the emergence and growth of organized animal protection. In a more specific way, however, the purpose of this work as a whole is to better understand the increases in both consumption of animal-based foods and in organized animal protection.

POPULATION AND FOOD

The current world population is over 6 billion, with this figure expected to double in less than 50 years (Population Reference Bureau 2004). The consensus among researchers is that the convergence of population growth, environmental problems, and the inherently limited nature of our basic resources, including land, water, and energy, all point to the urgent need for evaluation of resources in relation to the rapidly growing human population.

For the same amount of calories, a meat-based diet requires much more land, water, and energy resources than a more sustainable lactoovovegetarian diet (Pimentel and Pimentel 2003). Globally, livestock utilization of land resources will increase dramatically in the future driven by the exponentially expanding human population's growing demand for meat (Sere, Steinfeld and Groenewold 1996). This expansion of demand will include both extensive and intensive production, both of which in the past have led to increases in environmental degradation (United Nations 2001). The current shortage of productive cropland, a significant cause of global food shortages (Leach 1995), will be pushed toward an increasingly critical level as the demand for meat increases. Our use of land, in all matters, is an issue of undeniable importance.

Water is another resource that is fast becoming a global concern. The availability of adequate supplies of freshwater for human agricultural needs is critical in many regions of the world, with the worldwide per capita availability of water declining by 60% between 1960 and 1997 (Postel 1997). Livestock production can and has polluted water resources through slaughter waste, animal waste, and fertilizer contaminants used in growing feed (Barrett 2001; Delgado 1997). Both supply and quality of water worldwide will continue to be negatively impacted by increases in the use of animals as a food source.

As with land and water, the use of energy resources in animal-based food production is an issue of serious concern. For example, in the United States, the amount of fossil energy input required in animal protein production systems is more than 11 times greater than that the amount required for grain protein production (Pimentel and Pimentel 2003; United States Department of Agriculture 2004). Given that food production of any type will have to increase to feed a growing population, demands for energy to produce food will inevitably increase regardless of the specifics of diets around the globe. However, the fact that production of animal-based food requires so much more energy that production of plant-based food should figure prominently in all policy directed at food production.

PATTERNS OF FOOD PRODUCTION, DISTRIBUTION, AND CONSUMPTION

Since the nineteenth century, the production of animal-based food, in particular meat, has become increasingly industrialized and structured on the principles of mass production. An ever increasing trend towards efficiency, speed, and quantity has changed how animal-based food is produced, distributed, and consumed. Industrialized modernization brought fundamental changes in the interactions between socio-economic systems and the natural environment. In the production of meat, livestock management has increasingly shifted from grassland-based cattle farming and range grazing to intensive practices based in part on Fordist principles.

By the middle of the twentieth century, developed countries had created industrialized breeds, through innovations in environmental control, genetics, nutrition, and disease management, that were not only seen as efficiently transforming grains into higher value meat products, but could guarantee optimal outcome at the end of the production process (Boyd 2001). Eventually, these changes in production would be woven into culture, with such advertising icons as Elsie the Cow smiling benignly on mass-produced milk containers, representing the idyllic farm of the past, being overshadowed by the specter of unbridled modernization perhaps best seen in the repeated media images of spastic cattle suffering from BSI ("mad cow disease"). The modernization of meat production resulted in new breeds of animals, new uses of meat by-products, shifts in relationships between humans and animals, and often new and unanticipated risks and benefits to humans and non-humans alike.

The distribution of meat, like the production process, underwent dramatic changes beginning in the nineteenth century. Because of the efficient use of all parts of the animal, there was an increase in affordable meat-based products to all types of consumers. With the advances in technology, meat now had a longer shelf-life in all climates and locations, and could be transported by rail, then trucking, and eventually by air. Although the possibility of preserving food in airtight containers was discussed well before the apex of the industrial age, and the invention of canning was hastened by Napoleon's 1795 cash prize offering for innovations in meat preservation, the mass preserving of affordable meats did not truly begin until William Underwood began packing and selling his immensely popular Deviled Ham in the 1820s (Bryant 2003). Now, not only military personnel, but poor urban workers, and a much wider range of the world's population in general, were all consuming relatively inexpensive boiled, chopped, and ground meat and meat by-products. Hormel's Spam in the 1930s, followed by a variety of previously unimaginable forms of meat products, marks the ascendance of the affordable meat-based food, rising from the convergence of demand, technology, and consumers' perceptions of the value of meat (Lewis 2000).

Along with changes in production and distribution, consumption of animal-based foods changed radically since the nineteenth century. In Europe, for example, before 1800, meat was consumed by the aristocracy and upper classes, but only as an exception by other classes. The democratization of the consumption of meat began in the early nineteenth century, as the absence of meat came to be seen as a form of deprivation. Scientists and physicians emphasized the health benefits believed to come from meat, while the agricultural and industrial revolutions brought such advances as improved animal husbandry and fodder production, canning, and refrigeration (Knapp 1997).

On the other hand, consumer concerns regarding the suffering of livestock have become increasingly common since the nineteenth century, and livestock production, distribution, and processing practices that address consumer concerns regarding farm animals' quality of life have and will continue to evolve (Hughes 1995). An intriguing pattern has developed: during the twentieth century, developed countries have increased their consumption of meat across all socio-economic classes, with many of these countries also experiencing a concurrent increase in formal, organized efforts to protect from pain and suffering the very animals being processed and consumed.

EMERGENCE OF ANIMAL PROTECTION

Appearing during the Victorian Era, the concept of *animal rights* was firmly planted in the public mind by 1900. Grounded in humanitarian trends that had clearly manifested in the political realm by the beginning of the nineteenth century, Henry Salt's 1892 treatise *Animal Rights*, published in 1894, is the primary representative text in the emergent animal protection and rights ideology. Although vivisection was a concern, the most visible use of animal life involved the production and consumption of animals as food, a process involving factory farming, transportation to markets, and the inevitable carnage of the slaughterhouse, all increasingly noted by the public eye. Salt's statement that "everyone must satisfy himself of the necessity, the real necessity, of the use of flesh-food, before he comes to any intellectual conclusion on the subject of animals' rights" (Salt 1894:65) represents the ideology of animal rights that developed in response to the industrial slaughterhouse, rather than a century later in the *new social movements* of the 1970s as some social movement scholars have suggested. This response to the industrialization of meat originated in the same global discursive and epistemic communities that launched systematic critiques of existing social systems in the industrialized world.

Much of the nineteenth century advocacy literature was grounded in an argument for compassion and the reduction of suffering of animals as part of a larger movement for social progress. This rhetorical framing of animal protection continued throughout the twentieth century into the 1970s, and was used by humane societies that organized in developed countries as part of national, regional, and local publicly funded projects, as well as providing the philosophical foundation for works considered seminal to the contemporary animal rights movement.

Although the framing of grievances in animal advocate organizations usually are sorted into three distinct categories, those of *compassion, utilitarian logic*, or *inherent value*, all of these arguments are grounded in the assertion that animal protection is clearly inseparable from both social progress and a universally improved human condition. From the early nineteenth century works of such groups as English humane societies and anti-vivisectionists organizations, up through the early animal rights positions of the 1970s, most texts and rhetoric promoting animal protection was clearly grounded in compassion and the reduction of pain or suffering.

In the 1970s, Peter Singer, philosopher and academic, wrote *Animal Liberation : A New Ethics for Our Treatment of Animals* (1975) and several other works that became primary texts for the animal rights movement that was emerging from the broader, existing animal protection movement. Singer's approach is *utilitarian*: a being's worth should be calculated on concrete principles rather than membership in an abstract group, and *right* action is action that leads to the greatest good and the least amount of suffering. In this argument, animals have the same capacity for feeling and pain, therefore they deserve our consideration. Singer also brought attention to systematic animal suffering in factory farms and scientific research labs, describing in detail the conditions of both. Although Singer's position on reducing suffering is not the current definitive animal rights movement's position, his writing and work continues to be extremely influential in the fields of both animal protection and animal rights.

In the 1980s, a third grievance framing emerged, that of *inherent value*, with Tom Regan's early work usually being recognized as presenting the initial argument for this position (1982; 1983). By the 1990s, inherent value had become the definitive position of the animal rights movement, with many non-governmental organizations dedicated to animal protection adopting softened versions of inherent value into their own projects and definitions. Gary Francione, a professor at Rutgers Law School and director of Rutgers' Animal Rights Legal Clinic, is representative of the institutionalization of the inherent value position. Further developing Regan's initial framing of inherent value, Francione asserts that: 1) any attempt to balance animal and human interests with welfare laws will be futile; 2) property rights are the most valued rights by humans, and most animal-human conflicts arise over the use of animals as property; 3) therefore remove all laws that regulate animal use and initiate laws that prohibit animal use of any form by humans (1996; 2000). The non-human, then, has moved from status of protected property to that of protected individual, with this status being defined and supported by many formal social institutions.

Organizations dedicated to the protection of animals first appeared in nineteenth century England, building on eighteenth century treatises and discussions on pain and suffering. Animal protection and rights have typically appeared in countries that have experienced increased and democraticized meat consumption during the nineteenth and twentieth centuries as a result of the initial foray into implementing democratic principles. Institutionalizing over a century of interest in animal protection and individual animal rights, high-income countries and regions including Canada, United Kingdom, United States, European Union, and Australia, now lead the way in participants, legislation, and economic resources committed to a rapidly evolving inclusion of non-humans as right-bearing individuals in the political, social, cultural, economic, and moral spheres. The trend is that countries that are 1) considered high-income, 2) participate in construction of world culture, 3) make claims of being democratic, and 4) idealize individual rights, are countries that will be more likely to experience the emergence, growth, and institutionalization of organized animal protection efforts.

UNDERSTANDING MEAT CONSUMPTION AND ANIMAL PROTECTION

Modernization Theory

Modernization theory emerged in the 1950s as an explanation of the development of industrial societies, with an emphasis on the expansion of industrial capitalism beginning in the eighteenth century. Grounded in the assumption that societies develop in predictable stages, modernization theory asserts that development depends on the importation of technology and the knowledge needed to use it. In this theoretical model, increased levels of education, development of mass media and of democratic institutions, and the installation and improvement of both communication and transportation systems, are all characteristics of a stage of modernization (Rostow 1960). This theoretical approach presents modernization as a homogenizing and progressive process, characterized by eventually increased health and wealth for all members of the society.

During the twentieth century, the modernization of meat production in many countries was considered an indicator of social and economic progress, in that it made available to many that which had previously been available to very select groups (Franklin 1999). To a large extent, overall patterns of meat consumption reflect wealth more than food preferences, with animal foods being more expensive per calorie than plant foods (Grigg 1993; 1994; 1995b; 1999; 2001). This trend of increased wealth influencing meat consumption is often buttressed with research and rhetoric on health and nutrition that promotes the necessity of animal protein in the human diet. Modernization theory, with its assumptions of increased health and wealth as results of the modernization process, can help explain the steady increase in per capita meat consumption for all socio-economic classes in those countries considered modernized, as well as the lack of increase in those countries not modernized.

World-Systems Theory

Although emerging in the 1970s in part as a critical response to moderniza-tion theory, theoretical explanations that focus on world-systems share with modernization theory the premise of an expanding international economic system. However, world-systems theorists do not conceptualize development in terms of stages leading to beneficent modernization for all countries will-ing to modernize. Instead, countries fall into categories of core, semi-periph-ery, and periphery, with these categories being analogous to Marxist class cat-egories (Chirot and Hall 1982; Wallerstein 1966; 1979). Not only the distribution of wealth and resources are seen as being regulated by an inter-national capitalist world-system, but cultural, social, and political spheres are directly affected as well. Semi-peripheral and peripheral societies are depen-dent on the core industrialist nations that control wealth, technology, and mil-itary expertise. These core nations, then, have become the centers of wealth, development, and modernization, with their members experiencing the high-est standards of living, including increased consumption of the highly valued animal-based foods.

Theories of modernization and world systems can provide insights into the increases in meat consumption, but what about the concurrent increase in or-ganized animal protection?

World Society and World Culture

During the last hundred years, a concept of the world as a global social sys-tem has become increasingly prevalent. A single "international society" has emerged (Meyer 1987; Watson 1992), with individual and corporate actors viewing themselves as members and representatives of a world polity. This world polity is constituted and reproduced by a culture that provides models, patterns of behaviors, strategies, symbolic and ideological frames that shape and direct individual and corporate action. World culture, in this sense, refers to transnational cognitive paradigms and normative frameworks (Campbell 2002), and includes worldwide constructs that provide identities, selves, and roles that shape individual interests and actions. Collective identities and the interests of rational organizations, such as firms, states, and nations, are also defined through world-cultural conceptions (Boli and Thomas 1997). Far from being enacted mechanically, actors commonly enact world-cultural con-ceptions through innovative agency (Meyer and Jepperson 2000), with some theoretical analogies found in Peter Berger's ideas of the social construction of culture (Berger and Luckmann 1966) and in Bourdieu's concepts of *habitus* and of *cultural reproduction* (Bourdieu 1984; Bourdieu and Passeron 1977; Bourdieu and Thompson 1991).

Discussions of world society and world-cultural conceptions present contemporary constructed individual and corporate actors as organizing and legitimating themselves through universalistic models, including those of citizenship, socioeconomic development, and justice. These models are seen as pervasive at the world level, and involve consensus on ideas of human rights, the natural world, socioeconomic development, human health, and education. Often these models and shared ideas are seen as being universally applicable (Meyer et al. 1997). For example, standards of human health and nutrition, such as the minimum required fluid intake for infants, are consensually defined by such international entities as the United Nations and the World Health Organization, with these standards assumed to be universally applicable to all humans regardless of locale or region. Likewise, concepts such as basic human rights, world historic sites, protected species, and suffering in general, are all defined at the world level through highly rationalized, international associations premised on consensus.

World-cultural associations and conceptions have become increasingly important since the nineteenth century, and especially over the last hundred years, with a globally constructed definition of *social progress* emerging that includes an expanding definition of justice and rights. During this time, the number of international organizations dedicated to defining and implementing ideas of social progress, justice, and rights have been created at a rate that is more than just reflective of population increases and global economic expansion. Animal protection and rights, part of this discourse from the beginning, has become the responsibility of both corporate and individual actors who consider themselves, and desire to be considered by others, as members of a socially progressive society premised on contemporary ideas of justice and rights.

Chapter Two

Animal Protection and the Ideology of Progress

Although mythology, religion, and artifacts present many animals as divine, ideal, and creatures with moral status, much of recorded history provides evidence that humans have perceived non-human animals as subjects to be dominated, property to be owned, or objects to be consumed. When changes in philosophy, political organization, and law began moving towards recognition of individual rights, humanitarian principles, and a consensual idea of social progress, concepts of animal protection and rights also began to emerge as a characteristic of this idea of progress.

This chapter first examines how early religious and ethical belief systems regulated animal slaughter and the consumption of meat, and then moves into a discussion of the status of animals as redefined by scientific and philosophical communities in the eighteenth and nineteenth centuries. An overview of the changing social conditions and public perceptions that contributed to this change in the status of animals is also included.

Although this book does not argue in support or dismissal of any specific ideology of progress, careful attention is given to defining the idea of progress that emerged during the Enlightenment through the thought of such epistemic communities as the *Philosophes*, and related nineteenth century syntheses of notions of progress and theories of evolution. This idea of progress and related syntheses were essential to ideological assumptions that drove economic, political, and cultural expansion well under way by the eighteenth century. As later asserted by political reformers and social activists, nineteenth century ideas about the treatment and use of animals were directly related to changing ideas about dominion, individual rights, and social progress that had been developed within the philosophical and political revolutions of the eighteenth century.

Changes in the status of animals and the emergence of formal animal protection were but two of the many consequences of the development, support, and expansion of a world-level culture that defined the ideal society as one that shunned cruelty and violence, and promoted beneficent mastery of the natural world and all its creatures, as well as alleviate social and economic disparities among citizens. The purposes of this chapter include the identification and analysis of the early discourse and epistemic communities that defined progress and contributed to related changes in the status of animals, and to provide support and context for the explanations of social change and of world culture discussed throughout this work.

BEFORE ANIMAL PROTECTION

Early treatises exist that question the obvious violence that is an essential element of using animals for food purposes. Hesiod's *Works and Days*, from the eighth century BCE, associates a nonviolent, fleshless diet with the Golden Age of the past, an age superceded by a series of ages that are progressively violent and increasingly meat-based (Hesiod, Tandy and Neale 1996). This theme is developed even further through Pythagoras' religious and philosophical society established in Croton, Italy around 518 BCE. The Pythagorean inner circle of *mathematakoi* lived in a permanent communal arrangement that included no personal possessions and a strict vegetarianism (Riedweg 2005; Spencer 1996; Walters and Portmess 1999). Early biographers of Pythagoras, such as Ovid (43 BCE-CE 17), recount Pythagoras as objecting to meat-eating because it involves unwarranted violence against other living creatures, as well as being an impious habit with evil consequences for the immortal soul (Walters and Portmess 2001). Text fragments of the fifth-century BCE Pythagorean philosopher Empedocles describe animal sacrifice as a form of defilement, with the refusal to spill blood and vegetarianism viewed as necessary conditions for breaking the cycles of violence and returning to a peaceful Golden Age (Empedocles and Wright 1995).

Similarly, other religious and philosophical traditions have included a discussion of the ethics related to humans consuming other animals as food. The Vedic, Buddhist, Judaic, Christian, and Islamic traditions, all considered world-level belief systems, have texts and practices that either espouse ethical vegetarianism or provide support for adopting ethical vegetarianism. In the Vedic tradition, the earliest explicit writings on ethical vegetarianism are the *Laws of Manu* from the Epic Period (600 BCE-200 BCE) of Indian religious development. The *Laws of Manu* condemn all social and economic actions connected to meat eating as being spiritually impure, with a diet based on nonviolence offered as an essential element of ethical conduct (Manu and Jha 1999). Buddhist texts, emerging from the Vedic tradition as early as the first century BCE, continue the Vedic emphasis on ethical vegetarianism. As expressed in these early texts, spiritual liberation, or *Bodhi* enlightenment, is not possible for humans who eat the flesh of other living creatures (Balsys 2004; Phelps 2004).

The Judaic, Christian, and Islamic traditions, originating in areas inhospitable to agriculture and horticulture, are not overtly vegetarian, nor are the original spiritual leaders presented as forbidding the slaughter of animals for food. There are, however, contemporary threads of ethical vegetarianism grounded in the sacred texts of these traditions. Both Judaism and Islam produced laws, kosher and *halal*, governing the use of animals for food purposes, with some vegetarians in these traditions arguing that these laws were created to accommodate human bloodlust after the fall from a vegetarian Garden of Eden.

Within the Jewish tradition, some contemporary Talmudists argue that Genesis 9:3, "I now give you everything for food" is not a reversal, but rather a temporary concession to Genesis 1:29, which states "I give you every seed-bearing plant . . . and every tree that has fruit with seed in it. They will be yours for food." Rabbi Kook (1865-1935), one of the first clear defenders of ethical vegetarianism in the Jewish tradition, argued that human moral sense has developed to the point where justice should be demanded for all animals. The Garden of Eden is seen as the Golden Age, with the Fall from the Garden bringing with it violence and the forgetfulness of the sacred nature of all life (Kook 1978; Weitzman and Kook 1999). This line of thought is developed throughout the twentieth century, with subsequent scholars arguing for a pro-vegetarian bias in the Torah (Kalechofsky 1992), criticizing the brutalities of factory farming, and presenting meat-eating as violating the prohibition against killing (Pick 1977).

Although some individuals and a few sects within Christianity have viewed meat-eating as unethical, mainstream Christianity has shared Judaism's ambivalent approach to facing the contradiction between the slaughter and the sanctity of life. Historically, vegetarian Christian saints have objected to the eating of animals on the grounds that it indulges carnal appetite, not because of the spiritual consequences of killing another living creature nor the rights of the victim itself. As with Judaism, it was in the late nineteenth century that Christianity produced thinkers concerned with animal protection and rights, and even later in the twentieth century that Christian theologians began to formally include non-humans in a Christian model of justice. By the end of the twentieth century, Christian theologians had begun to define meat-eating in terms of institutional violence (Adams 1993), of a temporary concession that will be unnecessary in the future Kingdom of God (Linzey 1995), and of a utilitarianism that is contrary to God's original symbolic or literal Eden (Regan 1990).

Overall, Islam, as with the Abramic tradition in general, has not been directly concerned with the well-being of non-human animals. Although the killing of animals is forbidden within certain sacred sites, or *haraman*, and there are strict laws regarding animal slaughter, animal sacrifice continues to be part of Islamic holy feast days. A few individuals within Islam's mystical Sufi tradition have asserted that union with God includes practicing a spiritual love of all animals. This rare position is taught by the thirteenth century Sufi poet Rūmī, who warns that humans who slaughter animals for food are violating divine creation and love, and will experience retribution (Rūmī and Chittick 1983).

As with the tradition's historical Sufi scholars, contemporary Islamic scholars that question human use of animals as food are rare. Twentieth century writings include interpretation of Islamic law and parables that focus on compassion (Muhaiyaddeen 1985) and analysis of Islamic law and *Hadīth* that seeks to reduce cruelty and unnecessary taking of life (Masri 1987), but continue to be the exception within the Islamic tradition.

For centuries, the Vedic and Buddhist traditions have included a clear position on meat-eating as unethical, violent, and spiritually degrading. At the same time, these traditions did not take measures to protect or extend rights to non-human animals, rather they offered an ethical code of conduct that led to spiritual enlightenment or advancement of the soul. The Abramic traditions have never had an explicit command to refrain from meat-eating, and in fact, it was not until the twentieth century that Judaism, Christianity, and Islam began producing thinkers that addressed the protection and rights of animals.

CHANGES IN THE MORAL STATUS OF ANIMALS

By the beginning of the nineteenth century, animals were clearly becoming part of the human moral community, as objects in and of themselves. An early proponent of this position, English lawyer and utilitarian philosopher Jeremy Bentham (1748-1832) argued that both humans and animals have the capacity for suffering, and that this capacity is all that is required to substantiate a moral relationship between humans and animals. Animals not only suffer, and therefore are morally significant, but humans have moral obligations in all actions involving animals. (Bentham, Burns, and Hart 1996). Bentham's assertions are representative of the beginnings of a *humane treatment* principle that has supported moral and legal standards practiced since the nineteenth century, and they mark a clear departure from previous thought and practice in human relations with other animals. Earlier Cartesian thought had defined moral worth in terms of ability to reason, and much of religious thought and doctrine had defined non-humans as objects of dominion or property, but the humane treatment principle was based on the conceptualization of animals as beings who could suffer, feel pain, and were valuable as distinct individuals.

In the field of scientific investigation, Charles Darwin's work, as well as other nineteenth century work supporting ideas about biological and social evolution, proposed that differences between humans and other animals were differences of degree, rather than differences of type. Darwin argued that animals have many of the cognitive abilities and emotional responses that humans do, including love, memory, curiosity, maternal affection, and sympathy (Darwin 1981; Rachels 1999). Although *Origin of the Species* was not published until 1859, illustrated accounts of Darwin's voyages on the HMS *Beagle* influenced public perception as early as the 1830s (Kean 1998). As controversial as it was influential, the scientifically grounded kinship of all animals proposed by Darwin provided support for the humanitarian trend in nineteenth century legislation and collective social action.

During the nineteenth century, in Britain, on mainland Europe, and in Northern America, legislation, humane societies, and political organizations dedicated to animal protection had appeared and multiplied. These changes were driven by ideas of social progress and humanitarianism, and included a new conceptualization, proposed in both philosophy and science, of animals as distinct individuals with lives and feelings independent of their relationship to humans. In addition to the contributions from philosophy and science, the ideological base of organized animal protection was strengthened by a growing international network of radical social reformers that included Tolstoy, Gandhi, Clarence Darrow, George Bernard Shaw, and others involved in social and humanitarian movements.

Henry Salt, an active participant in this growing network, was a prolific writer and advocate for the social reform of prisons, schools, economic institutions, and the status of animals. His earlier articles, in the 1870s and 1880s, addressed land reform, criticized London's social policy and treatment of poverty, drew attention to the exploitation and vulnerability of workers, and raised questions about the causes of crime (Clark and Foster 2000). Salt, an economic materialist, promoted both socialism and vegetarianism, believing both would move societies toward a more humane world. In 1891, he founded the Humanitarian League, an organization dedicated to ending cruelty through systematic protest and social critique (Hendrick 1977), followed soon after by the publication of *Animal Rights: Considered in Relation to Social Progress* (Salt 1894).

Salt asserts that all animals have moral purpose and a sense of individuality, using the work of Schopenhauer and Darwin as support. Salt agrees with Schopenhauer's assertion that realizing one's true self is the highest moral purpose of both human and animal, as well as Schopenhauer's position against Cartesian ontology:

> The unpardonable forgetfulness in which the lower animals have hitherto been left by the moralist of Europe is well known. It is pretended that beasts have no rights. They persuade themselves that our conduct in regard to them has nothing to do with morals, or (to speak the language of their morality) that we have no duties towards animals; a doctrine revolting, gross, and barbarous. (Schopenhauer [1841]1903:23)

As further support for the principle of individual and animal rights, Salt often cites scientists convinced of animals' sense of individuality, represented in Darwin's statement "the senses and intuitions, the various emotions and faculties . . . of which man boasts, may be found in an incipient, or even sometimes well-developed condition, in the lower animals" (Darwin 1874; Salt 1894).

Both the philosophical position on moral status and the scientific position on individuality found in Salt's representative work on early animal rights show a clear break with the religious and Cartesian concepts of *being*, as well as the science informed by those concepts, that were prevalent before the nineteenth century. Throughout the nineteenth century, epistemic communities emerged that accepted the extended definition of morality represented in Schopenhauer's work, the scientific understanding of graduated individuality proposed by evolutionists such as Darwin, and the concept of animal rights found in Salt's work. These epistemic communities, which generated new ideas that constitute a world-level culture (Haas 1992; Keck and Sikkink 1998), promoted a change in the status of animals and provided the ideological motivation for organized and institutionalized animal protection.

THE CONTEXT OF PUBLIC PERCEPTION

The use of animals for food has been a source of concern to animal advocates since the beginning of the movement, and was very present in the nineteenth century public mind. As the production of meat became more industrialized and the demand for meat increased, the process of production itself increasingly became the object of public scrutiny. While the status of animals was being redefined in epistemic communities, almost all people living in industrialized countries witnessed a distinct shift from the idyllic *peaceable king-*

dom of the country farm to the metal-framed, concrete, cramped, industrial complexes that processed living creatures into standardized packages of meat. Although vivisection and blood sport were concerns of early animal advocates, citizens of industrialized countries were much more likely to be confronted regularly with situations related to the use of animals for food purposes.

Animals had been sold and slaughtered in urban market settings for centuries, and the business of butchery had always been a source of public concern. However, the arrival and consequences of industrialism, combined with dramatic increases in urban populations, created demands that overwhelmed the urban market of centuries past and increasingly brought people into physical contact with the realities of animal slaughter. Motivated by the ideology of social progress shaped by science, philosophy, and industrialism, the market slaughterhouses were criticized as unhygienic, demoralizing, and inefficient.

The Smithfield cattle market had existed on the edge of London for centuries, with animals being driven through London's streets weekly for the cattle auctions held every Monday and Friday. By the nineteenth century, London had engulfed Smithfield, giving citizens of London daily opportunities to see cattle handled by the market's drovers responsible for the final days of the animals' lives (Bonser 1970). By the 1820s, the refuse and cruelty of the butchers' shambles was protested by reformers, such as those who wrote in *Voice of Humanity* that the animal market conditions in London were "highly disgraceful to one of the largest, most populous and richest capitals in the universe" (1827:2), suggesting in a series of editorials and essays that London was not meeting the standards of a socially progressive nation. In most industrialized countries, urban growth had created conditions similar to those seen in London's Smithfield market, prompting emerging ideas regarding social progress and civilized urban life to be enacted.

Reformers advocated the establishment of public slaughterhouses that would reduce animal suffering, address sanitation issues, and remove slaughter from the view of urban public society, and by the 1870s, London's cattle trade was conducted mostly in the newly built rail yards outside of London (Perren 1978). Beginning in 1822, Parliament had enacted legislation specifically aimed at protecting farm animals and regulating slaughter. Around this same time, Paris, Vienna, Brussels, and Berlin were among many European towns and cities that established public facilities in the industrial outskirts, with these facilities being regulated and administered by the state and open only to licensed butchers and personnel (Brantz 2002).

In late nineteenth century North America, slaughter was becoming offensive to growing urban populations, with the protection of animals from cruelty advocated by urban elites. Founded in 1866 by wealthy citizens of New York City, the American Society for the Prevention of Cruelty to Animals lobbied and convinced the New York state legislature to pass the nation's first anti-cruelty laws, with specific attention to farm and work animals (Carson 2003). Soon after in 1869, the Canadian Society for the Prevention of Cruelty to Animals was founded in Montreal in 1869 by a group of prominent citizens, with assistance from anti-cruelty societies in Paris, England, and the United States (Canadian Society for the Prevention of Cruelty to Animals 1873).

Nineteenth century ideas about the treatment and use of animals were directly related to changing ideas about dominion, individual rights, and social progress that had been developed within the philosophical and political revolutions of the eighteenth century. The ideas and texts that had provided ideological bases for the revolutions that sought to institutionalize individual rights and social progress were likewise the foundation of organized animal protection. In less than a hundred years, animals had become individuals capable of suffering and legally deserving of protection from cruelty. Informed by epistemic communities, early organized animal protection was advocated by social and economic elites, and encoded at the national level. Public perception was involved, in that educated citizens in developed urban areas were no longer willing to tolerate visible slaughter or cruelty towards animals. The educational models, dispersed and enforced by epistemic communities, aimed at instilling democratic principles and concepts of social progress, and emphasized ideas about what was civilized and humane. Although there was still resistance to extending individuality to non-humans, animals were well on their way to inclusion in universalistic models of social progress and justice, with animal protection as a characteristic of social progress becoming the norm.

THE IDEA OF PROGRESS

The ideas of the Enlightenment were essential to the radical, societal transformation that was taking place at the end of the eighteenth century (Coleman 1993). Breaking with the underlying ideology of established political and social institutions, Enlightenment thinkers emphasized the ability of human reason to dispel ignorance, the ability of philosophical and scientific progress to improve society, the importance of knowledge, and the importance of liberty and equal treatment before the law for all members of society. In support of promoting these most promising ideals, there was a growing attention to social context: social, political, and legal institutions could provide the environment that shaped interactions between individuals and institutions in the most beneficial way (Wood 1992), with the highest path being that which led to the greatest good for the greatest number of societal members. For the most part, Enlightenment thinkers' ideas about *social good* emerged from their philosophical utilitarianism, and their commitment to natural law, socialism and democratic principles (Gay 1954). The assertion of the universality of human nature and goals, as well as the existence of universal benevolence as a prescription of naturally based ethics, were also characteristic of Enlightenment thought (Shimony 1997).

The idea of progress itself asserts that humanity has advanced in the past, is advancing now, and will continue to advance in the future, with an overall trend towards improvement (Nisbet 1980). As presented in Enlightenment thought, social progress is the result of systematic application of reason and science to society. Although by no means subscribing to a fundamentalist Cartesian rationalism, Enlightenment thinkers, including Locke, Voltaire, Bayle, Rousseau, Lessing, and Kant all agreed that reason provided the guide for ultimate value, and led to certain ethical conclusions regarding the dignity and rights of individuals as essential to social progress (Iggers 1965). In short, *social progress* is the notion that all experience is directed toward the future with the specific, calculated purpose of improving or bettering the world, society, and the individual. As eventually suggested in the work of such social theorists as Comte, Marx, and Spencer, social progress itself could be not only an object of scientific inquiry, but could be rationally planned.

During the eighteenth and nineteenth centuries, social progress became a dominant idea, providing the eventual grounds for animal protection, as well as the essential concepts of social justice and humanitarianism. The *Philosophes*, beginning in the mid-eighteenth century, presented the clearest and earliest collective expression of the ascendancy of social progress as an organizing principle. *Philosophe* was an expression circulated by the French, and defined in Diderot's *Encyclopedia*, a new kind of philosopher: cosmopolitan, humanist, a persuasive and lucid writer and clearly not associated either with the Church or the university. In an essay titled *"Philosophe"* in Diderot's *Encyclopedia*, the *philosophe* is one who

> trampling on prejudice, tradition, universal consent, authority, in a word all that enslaves most minds, dares to think for himself, to go back and search for the clearest general principles, to admit nothing except on the testimony of his experience and his reason. (Diderot and Alembert [1751]1965:321)

As an epistemic community, the *Philosophe* movement included a decidedly French core of Montesquieu, Rousseau, Diderot, and Voltaire, but as quickly as ideas could be dispersed and shared, it was soon enveloping influential thinkers such as David Hume, Cesare Beccaria, Benjamin Franklin, and Thomas Jefferson. The *Philosophes* defined progress in terms of advancement of knowledge and technology, the elimination of ignorance generated by superstition and religions, and overcoming human cruelty and violence through improving both social conditions and governments. Intentional, rational advances in these areas would most likely lead to beneficent mastery of the natural world and peaceful human relations.

Written in 1740, Voltaire's *Essai sur les moeurs et l'esprit des nations* suggested that the growth of the sciences, arts, morals and laws, commerce and industry were all indications of progress. Ignorance, however, led to individuals and nations engaging in irrational conflicts and cruel impositions. If the ignorance and prejudices manifest in wars and religions were extinguished, then the barriers to social progress, and thus improvement, would be removed (Voltaire [1740]1975). For Voltaire, as with most *Philosophes*, the human faculty of reason, interlaced with the practice of justice and pity deemed essential to human life, was the key to progress, as well as the cure for ignorance and cruelty. Social progress required reforming or replacing existing political, economic, and cultural systems, with the intention being to dispel ignorance on all counts and creating societies based on consent.

Diderot, sharing Voltaire's views regarding social progress and prolific dispersion of ideas and knowledge in general through dialogue and writing, produced numerous articles, the *Encyclopedia* (1751). as well as experimental fiction. The *Philosophe* critical approach marks even the pedestrian histories produced by Diderot, as in his description of the British constitution's development as a series of long and violent crises that resulted in a constitution with real disadvantages, but still the best outcome given the circumstances (Diderot [1751]1977).

Rousseau's thought, sometimes interpreted as compromising individual rights in service of the *general will*, is, however, representative of the *Philosophe* conceptualization of social progress that would be so influential in the ideology of animal protection, with his work likewise playing a prominent role in the revival of classical rights theory in twenty-first century political thought (Scott and Zaretsky 2003). His emphasis on equality as essential to social progress is found throughout his writings, and is reflective of the *Philosophe* epistemic community. In his *Social Contract*, Rousseau identifies inequality as the prime evil, explains how inequality developed, and in a section written initially for Diderot's *Encyclopedia*, provides an outline of the specific political order required to eliminate all forms of inequality. Rousseau asserts that interdependent need and private property resulted in the rise of inequality, and that the social progress achieved in previous ages was thus interrupted (Rousseau [1762]1997). Although an arguably romanticized communal utopia emerges in Rousseau's depiction of the past, his suggestion for future progress is not a return to the past, but rather the establishment of a social order that eliminates the conditions leading to inequality.

The *Philosophes'* concept of progress included the necessity of equality and a supporting view of justice, a critical view of social conditions, an emphasis on ignorance and cruelty as the most significant barriers to progress, and a radical reconsideration of the political rights of individuals and collectives. As an epistemic community, they were decidedly synthesists, crossing not only disciplinary boundaries, but national and geographic barriers as well. By definition, as an epistemic community, there was a shared understanding of the meaning of social progress, whether among the core *Philosophe* members, the philosophy of Hume or Beccaria, or the thought and revolutionary efforts of Franklin and Jefferson. During the *siècle des lumières* of the *Philosophes*, Paris was the destination of all of these individuals at one time or another, both through travel and their prolific epistolary exchanges, and likewise invitations were extended for travel outside of France (Hulliung 1994).

Although fiery exchanges, deep misunderstandings, and curious interactions did occur between core and peripheral members of the *Philosophe* community, such as Rousseau's stay at Hume's home-Rousseau expecting discipleship, Hume merely offering shelter and hospitality (Ages 1999)—overwhelmingly they all shared an idea of progress. David Hume viewed inequality as an impediment to social progress, not just among individuals, but among nations ([1752]1963). Hume criticizes both sentimentalism and extreme rationalism, and argues that the extended and extensive human sentiment of sympathy or benevolence is a natural human quality that underlies social order ([1751]1998). This natural benevolence combined with the free and critical use of human intellect is the essence of progress for Hume. This belief in the relationship between human advancement, equality, and the intellecutal and moral authority of the individual also underlies the political thought of Franklin, Jefferson and other American *Philosophes*. Overall, whatever their country of origin, the members of this epistemic community defined progress as a consequence of rational inquiry, and inseparable from a ceaseless critique of the state of human knowledge, of society and politics, and of necessity involving equality, justice, and benevolence, as well as the increased concern for alleviation of suffering in individual and collective forms.

The *Philosophes* generated and supported ideas about dominion, individual rights, and social progress that led to dramatic change during the eighteenth century. During the nineteenth century, ideas about social progress that had been developed in eighteenth century epistemic communities continued to gain momentum and continued to affect change, including a conceptualization of social progress that would so strongly contribute to the ideological base of organized animal protection. In the fields of political theory, social science, and biology, the idea of progress, as a fact and a possibility, was becoming a guiding principle. Whether in its continued importance in reforming political institutions, in its role in theories proposed in the emerging social sciences, or in the evolutionary models being proposed in biology, the idea of progress continued to be defined and refined in nineteenth century epistemic communities, which in turn shaped political thought and legislation, and thus everyday interactions between individuals.

In the political practice of the nineteenth century, social progress was increasingly understood in terms of equality, elimination of violence and cruelty, and dispersion of social justice. Developments in biological science and the emerging field of sociology provided both apparent evidence and systematic theories for measuring and engineering progress. In the field of biology, theories of evolution led to a concept of universal kinship, albeit one of degree, that challenged existing understandings of the moral status of all creatures. The emerging social sciences were now offering new visions of human purpose and of society that were grounded in assumptions about progress and all that it entailed.

The nineteenth century inherited from the previous not only radical changes in political theory, practice, and structure, the related revolutions, and the elimination of monarchial power, but also an emerging discourse on evolution that changed human relations with other animals. In the early eighteenth century, Linnaeus' taxonomy classified humans as part of the Primate order (Linne [1735]1964), and it had become widely accepted that animals had nervous systems similar to those of humans (Thomas 1983). By the time Darwin asserted that the difference in mind between man and the higher animals, although great, was one of degree and not of kind (Darwin [1871]1936), the protection of animals as a measure of social progress had already begun. What Darwin's and works similar to his did was provide support for the growing belief that animals were moral and physical kin to humans, and thus inherently worthy of protection.

In the late eighteenth century, evolutionary principles were presented and supported with evidence from the natural world (Corsi 2005; Herbert 2005). The taxonomy of the Swedish botanist Linnaeus included assumptions about the mutability of species, and similarly the French naturalist Comte de Buffon presented work on the connection between use and retention of organs in vertebrates. Both of these early works on evolution suggested that humans and apes are related, and that all living creatures have a common ancestor (Buffon [1749]2000; Linne [1735]1964). The naturalist Jean Lamarck, an associate of Buffon, furthered these ideas and presented a fully developed theory of the evolutionary origins of species ([1809]1984). By the time of the HMS *Beagle* voyages in the 1830s, the ideas recorded in Darwin's private notebooks on *transmutation of the species* and his metaphor of *the tree of life* were still considered radical, but they were supported by a transnational community of scientists, as well as several political and social theorists (Dennett 1995).

Evolutionary theory, as presented by naturalists and biologists, added a scientific voice in support of the idea of progress. Humans presumably were the most highly evolved species, successful both in terms of being the fittest and extremely adaptable, and the most capable of modifying, controlling, and improving the world. On the other hand, a scientifically constructed kinship of species suggested that humans were the most evolved by degree, not by type, with progress or improvement possible for all lesser evolved species (Hull 2005). Not confined to the circles of naturalists and biologists, theories of evolution were also developed in the social sciences. As in other scientific fields, theories of evolution and related ideas of progress were being developed in the emerging social sciences.

Social theorists integrated principles of evolutionary theory into their ideas of social progress. Evolutionary theory can be seen in Comte's *Law of Human Progress*, was essential to Spencer's social Darwinism, and was implied in Marx's historical materialism. Comte attempted to explain societal change in evolutionary language, and frequently stated that intellectual evolution was the preponderant principle of his explanation of human progress (Comte and Martineau [1853]2001). Spencer, using the evolutionary term *survival of the fittest*, viewed progress in terms of environmental pressures forcing individuals and collectives to improve in order to survive (Jones 1980). Marx's theories of social change, although distinct from strictly Darwinian concepts of evolutionary change (Geoffrey 1992), clearly presented an adaptive process contingent on struggle and environment. In Marx's historical materialism, struggle is the engine of progress, fed by human ability to harness the forces of nature.

The idea of progress, emerging in the eighteenth century and further developed in the nineteenth, was conceptualized within several epistemic communities. Philosophers, naturalists, biologists, social theorists, and others, within their respective disciplines as well as through interdisciplinary efforts, provided a frame of reference for the emergence of organized animal protection. Public perception, in response to new ideas generated and dispersed by epistemic communities, in response to changing normative beliefs, and in response to the environmental pressures of swelling human populations, eventfully led to increased support for organized animal protection.

The ideology of early organized animal protection was grounded in the discourse on progress that had been built since the eighteenth century. Ideas about equality, property, political authority, individual rights, and principles of evolution had all come to be seen as elements of progress, with progress being presented frequently in a favorable light as both the rational and natural improvement of human society. Likewise the reduction of suffering and violence, and the development of social justice came to be seen as elements of a rational, evolved humanitarianism. Throughout the nineteenth century, a growing number of citizens' groups, humanitarian organizations, and politicians sought to improve society by advocating animal protection. Their arguments were grounded in an ideology of progress that had led to democratic revolutions, to changes in individual and property rights, to the creation of social justice, and to the practice of organized humanitarian intervention.

What had been speculation in the 1780s would become practice over the next few decades. In *An Introduction to the Principles of Morals and Legislation*, Jeremy Bentham clearly phrased animal protection in terms of extending rights:

> The day may come when the rest of the animal creation may acquire those rights which never could have been withheld from them but by the hand of tyranny. . . . The time will come when humanity will extend its mantle over everything that breathes. ([1789]1907:310)

During the nineteenth century, many epistemic communities would echo Bentham's statement in their continuous definition of animal protection as an indicator of social progress. Once developed, the concept of animal protection would continue to spread globally with the expansion of a world-level culture that defined the ideal society as one that attempted to eliminate cruelty and violence.

Chapter Three

Increased Meat Consumption and the Ideology of Progress

Patterns of meat consumption change as societies modernize, and are influenced by a variety of social phenomena and environmental pressures. Many have argued that the origin of the human species is a consequence, in part, of early hominids' opportunities for scavenging and killing of grassland animals. Although arguably a nutritional necessity for evolving increased brain size, meat has typically not been a staple in human diets. In many pre-industrial societies, the labor power of animals has been more valued than their meat, with meat-eating permitted only during rare circumstances and only for a select few, as exemplified in much of India's history (Harris 1965). Similarly, in medieval Britain, oxen were traditionally not eaten because they were too important in agricultural tasks (Dyer 1988; Harvey 1993). Beginning in the early nineteenth century, countries that were modernizing and eliminating animal labor power experienced both the modernization of meat production and the democratization of meat consumption.

Meat consumption has increased globally for the last two centuries, with the most dramatic increases seen in those countries that industrialized early. In the twentieth century, when development has become pervasive, a majority of countries have experienced increased meat consumption, with some differences in rates, and core countries experiencing the highest increase in rates. Interestingly, some surveys show that the rate of meat consumption has begun to decline among certain socio-economic groups in some countries (Richardson, MacFie and Shepherd 1994). However, such surveys should be considered in light of statistics that show continued increase in annual per capita meat supply, as well as increases in calories per capita per day supplied by meat, in a majority of countries, with the greatest increases most often found in developed or wealthy countries (Food and Agriculture Organization of the United Nations 2005).

This chapter begins with an overview of meat-eating in human societies, leading into a discussion of the increased consumption of meat by the general population, not just elite groups, clearly evident during the nineteenth century. By the twentieth century, meat consumption was further developed as an ideological component of progress, manifest in theories and practices of economic development, modernization, and overall health of populations, with sharply increasing meat consumption becoming a global phenomenon. As part of the analysis of twentieth century increases in meat consumption, both statistical data and relevant theories of modernization and development are examined. Although theories of modernization and development can explain changes at the societal level, as well as support the idea that consumption of meat is an indicator of socio-economic improvement, they do not critically address the underlying assumptions supporting the ideological emphasis on progress.

This ideology of progress, a belief that all experience is or should be directed towards a future with the specific, calculated, purpose of improving world, society, and individual, is an element of world-level culture. At the same time that the consumption of meat was increasing and becoming democratized, the status of animals was being redefined, with both being grounded in an ideology of progress. Both increased meat consumption and formal animal protection occurred as part of the expansion of world-level culture.

EATING MEAT

Evidence suggests that humans have eaten meat throughout their existence as a species. According to studies in human evolution, the hominid family, beginning about 2.2 million years ago, developed a branch that had decreased molar size, less mandibular and cranial robusticity, alterations in incisor shape, greater cranial capacity, and reduced gut size. Many researchers from diverse scientific fields believe this suggests that animal foods played a prominent role in the development of larger brains in hominids, and led to the emergence of early humans (Crawford 1992; Demment, Young and Sensenig 2003; Larsen 2003; Milton 2003).

Early evidence of agriculture dates from around 12,000 years ago, and marks the beginning of cultivated grains in the human diet. Agrarian societies were well established by 3000 BCE, from which time there is continuous evidence of the dramatic increase of rice, corn and wheat in human diets (Johnson and Earle 2000; Lenski and Lenski 1987). On all major continents, agrarian societies emerged and dominated for thousands of years, with the human diet reflecting this in a heavy dependence on cultivated grains, with meat being valued more highly and as an occasional food. In some cases, as in the Vedic tradition, an increasingly plant-based diet was supported by an ideology that allowed meat-eating only for a select, elite few, with dire spiritual consequences for violators (Harris 1965). Meat-eating was also regulated in the Abramic traditions (Fabre-Vassas 1997), either through strict dietary laws as in Judaism and Islam (Lapidus 1988), or later through mandatory fasting and prohibitions in Christianity (Adamson 2004).

In the Western medieval diet, meat was regulated by the Church and state, including specific days for fasting and for eating fish. A study of the diet of a Westminster Benedictine monastery in London from 1100 to 1540 provides some insight into the consumption of meat during the Middle Ages and early modern Europe. The Benedictines not only owned a great deal of property, but eventually enjoyed the same diet as nobility, gentry or urban elites living outside of the cloister. Consumption of fish, flesh-meat, and meaty-dishes, as well as all other types of food eaten, were recorded in separate categories. In the monastery's early years, meat was reserved for the ill, but by 1500, monastery records indicate an average of 908 grams (c. 2 lbs.) of flesh-meat alone per monk on regulated meat days, which numbered around 75 days a year (Harvey 1993). Even though religious thought and doctrine during this time clearly described meat as having deleterious effects on the body and the soul, it was consumed in large quantities by socially and economically privileged groups, including the Benedictines.

During the European Middle Ages in general, there was a great difference in quality, quantity, and variety between the diets of a small, wealthy elite and of the population in general (Fenton and Kisban 1986; Pullar 1970). As best as historians can tell, admittedly with the habits of elites being most documented well into the eighteenth century, only the wealthy, powerful elite groups have eaten meat regularly and frequently in agrarian societies, including Europe from the Middle Ages to the early eighteenth century.

Meat was a symbol of wealth and status, even when the feast of the Middle Ages was replaced by the dinner party of early modernity. Two English dinner party menus, recorded in 1662 and 1663, consisted of carp, roasted chickens, salmon, oysters, rabbit hash, a lamb, and beef (Pepys [1660–69]1970). Even greater demonstrations of meat consumption were displayed by monarchs and other political elites, such as the Prussian Frederick the Great and his guests, who reportedly consumed in a single meal more chicken, beef, lamb, sausage, veal, mutton, goose, turkey, and other meats than most peasants ate in a lifetime (Haenel 1988). For La Mancha aristocrats, records indicate that meat was the most important food, consumed daily, in variety, and accounting for at least 43 per cent of total food expenditure (Sarasua 2001). As with the earlier English Benedictines, Ursuline nuns in eighteenth century France enjoyed a relatively upper class diet that frequently included beef, veal, mutton, and pork (Vedel 1975).

The historical documents that do include observations on lower socio-economic groups, usually record that meat was not a regular item outside of elite groups nor for most of society. In the 1690s, British aristocrat William Petty noted that Irish peasants seldom ate meat (Fitzmaurice 1895; Petty [1656]1997). Around the same time, Parisian artisans and the working poor subsisted on meatless diets, with the latter group close to starvation. A few years later, a French traveler in 1709 noted that rural peasants in Auvergne, Sologne, and Champagne had eaten little or no meat for entire year (Bernard 1970).

William Stark, a physician observing conditions in eighteenth century Scotland, reported that people living around Inverness never had meat, eggs, or dairy in their diets (1788). In 1787, an Anglican priest focused on the eating habits of agricultural workers in Berkshire, and although not entirely meatless, their diet was similar to their counterparts in other regions and countries. The 32 Berkshire workers included in the study averaged about two ounces of meat per week for each individual (Davies [1795]1977). Until the beginning of the nineteenth century, rural agricultural workers, as well as urban artisans and the working poor, ate very little meat or no meat-based foods, or none at all.

Early in the nineteenth century, a relatively meatless diet was increasingly viewed as a form of economic and nutritional deprivation. Social activists and members of the scientific and medical communities, as well as those from other fields, framed the meatless diet as yet another way in which the working class and the poor were exploited. The radical English journalist William Cobbett, who frequently wrote on social and economic hardships endured by the working class and poor, noted that the workers who raised and tended animals used for food had in fact little or no meat in their diets ([1853]2001).

In the writings of Frederich Engels, diet was likewise seen as a form of worker deprivation, in that most of the working class lived on potatoes and other starches supplemented only rarely with meat ([1845]1993). Physicians throughout Europe in the nineteenth century wrote of the necessity of meat in the human diet, with protein increasingly identified as the necessary ingredient (Pereira 1843; Smith 1864). In addition to physicians promoting meat consumption, scientists produced findings, such as those by chemists on amino acids, that supported the necessity of meat in the human diet, and not just for a few, but for the entire population (Kamminga and Cunningham 1995).

Social institutions, including hospitals, prisons, and municipalities, began early in the nineteenth century practicing the ideas, philosophies, and theories that supported the democratization of meat consumption. In many countries in Europe, national health ministries began instructing hospitals to provide meat to patients daily (Lane 2001), penal systems increased meat in prison inmates' diets (Johnston 1985), and meat was included in food distributed to urban poor (Abel 1972; 1986).

Although precise longitudinal data on workers' meat consumption does exist for this time, the overall trend seems to have been that of significantly increased meat for workers over the course of the nineteenth century, verified in writings and comments of contemporaries (Booth [1899]1970; Hartwell 1961; Le Play 1982; Neild 1841; Pollard 1959). Especially after the 1850s, formal institutions and organizations in industrializing countries in Europe supported the increased consumption of meat for all members of society. This trend accelerated with changes in technology, organization of production, and land usage.

EATING MORE MEAT

Although statistical data on diet composition in the early nineteenth century is limited, evidence suggests that the predominantly poor populations of Europe began the century on diets of starchy staples, with meat providing little or none of their daily calories (Grigg 1995a). By the middle of the nineteenth century, not only had much of Europe overcome the problem of famine (Scholliers and Vandenbroeke 1982; Teuteberg 1975), but had undergone the ideological and technological shifts necessary for rapid and mass dietary changes. By late nineteenth century, the modernization of meat production, including such developments as refrigeration, canning, railways, factory farming, and industrial slaughterhouses, made meat and novel meat products increasingly available to the populations of developed countries. The countries participating in these beginnings of modern mass consumption included industrialized or wealthy European countries, the territories they had culturally and economically colonized, and those areas that provided the vast range lands required for livestock production.

As a result of the colonization and development of the Americas and Australia, there was little difficulty meeting the increased demands for meat from countries undergoing economic and technological modernization at the end of the nineteenth century. The range lands were either available or in the process of being cleared, and innovations in transportation, canning, and refrigeration were constant. For at least 600 years prior to industrialization, farms in Europe had been small scale with mixed usage, with changes being constrained by several factors. It was only through the extensive ranching and grazing practices, possible on much of the land taken by European colonization of the Americas, Africa, and Australia, that the increased demands and perceived protein shortages of the late nineteenth century could be supplied and addressed (Rifkin 1992).

In the United States, there were dramatic increases in cattle production by the 1860s, and by the 1870s these increases were supplying not only growing urban populations in the United States, but also being imported by Britain, where Parliament was expressing formal concerns about protein shortages (Bartrip 1985; Paulus 1974). Over the next few decades, Australia, Argentina, and the United States, utilizing canning, chilling, freezing, and innovations in transportation, all competed to supply Europe's growing demands for meat.

As economic conditions for workers improved, and the professional and service classes expanded, an increased percentage of individual, household and national budgets were spent on meat and animal-based foods. In Germany, per capita per annum consumption of meat in 1816 was 16 kg, but had increased to 51 kg in 1907 (Teuteberg 1971), while French consumption of meat increased from 117 calories per capita per day in 1803–1812 to 275 calories in 1894–1904 (Grigg 1995a). In Belgium, beginning clearly with the innovations of the 1860s and 1870s, meat consumption increased from 15 kg per capita per annum in 1880 to 60 kg in 1960 (Scholliers and Vandenbroeke 1982). Countries such as the United States, Australia, Argentina, and New Zealand not only supplied meat to large population centers in wealthy countries, but had very meat-rich diets in the late nineteenth century, a trend that continued throughout the twentieth century.

Small scale production, such as ranges and pastures, were replaced by intensive factory farming systems constructed in proximity to grain producing areas. As meat production became increasingly modernized, it claimed a growing influence on economies. By the beginning of the twentieth century the rise in meat consumption was becoming globalized, with both developed and developing countries being urged to incorporate animal-derived protein into diets on a mass scale. Nutritionists, agricultural agencies, social welfare advocates, national governments, and commercial corporations all supported the consumption of meat as a marker of health and wealth.

MEAT CONSUMPTION IN THE TWENTIETH CENTURY

Meat consumption at the end of the nineteenth century had increased most dramatically in both the countries that were demanding more meat and the countries supplying the increasing demand. During the twentieth century increases in meat consumption were seen globally, with even those countries culturally predisposed against meat-eating and categorized as low income experiencing increases, albeit at a lesser rate than wealthy countries. Based on analysis of the United Nations Food and Agriculture Organization data collected globally, the main determinant of per capita meat consumption appears to be wealth (Speedy 2003). Globally, meat consumption and supply increased with incomes, peaking for developed countries in the 1980s when one third of all calories consumed came from livestock products (Grigg 1994).

Surveys and reported statistics on meat consumption became increasingly available in the twentieth century, with the Food and Agriculture Organization of the United Nations providing the most exhaustive and global statistics related to human food supply and consumption. These statistics, covering the last half of the twentieth century (1961–2002), show a continuation of historical patterns of consumption described in various sources prior to the establishment of standardized, global methods of data collection and reporting. At the world aggregate level, meat supply per capita per year (table 1) increased from 23 kg in 1961 to 39.3 kg in 2002, and meat-supplied calories per capita per day increased from 109.5 in 1961 to 217.1 in 2002 (table 2).

Table 1. Meat Supply Per Capita Per Year, 1961–2002

	Meat Supply Per Capita Per Year (kg)	
Aggregate and Country	*1961*	*2002*
World	23	39.3
Western Europe	53.5	91
Industrialized countries	58	93.3
Australia	103.9	108.8
New Zealand	107.4	106.7
United States	88.7	124.1
Latin America and Caribbean	33.8	61.2
Argentina	102.1	96.4
Paraguay	71.9	70.3
Uruguay	107.8	77.7
Low income countries	. . .	. . .
Bangladesh	3.2	3.1
Cambodia	4.9	13.9
Gambia	10.6	5.2
India	3.7	5.2
Indonesia	3.5	8.2
Nigeria	7.9	8.6
Rwanda	4.0	4.4

Source: Food and Agriculture Organization of the United Nations 2005.

Table 2. Meat-Supply Calories Per Capita Per Day

Aggregate and Country	Meat-Supplied Calories Per Capita Per Day	
	1961	2002
World	109.5	217.1
Western Europe	267	428.3
Industrialized countries	255.4	387.8
Australia	515.5	462
New Zealand	485.6	457.6
United States	335.1	452.5
Latin America and Caribbean	178.1	288.4
Argentina	646.1	557.1
Paraguay	262.1	296.1
Uruguay	678.9	442.3
Low income countries	. . .	. . .
Bangladesh	14.8	13.4
Cambodia	31.3	101.8
Gambia	50.5	24.1
India	15.8	23.1
Indonesia	20.8	46.2
Nigeria	35.3	39.7
Rwanda	17.5	20.7

Source: Food and Agriculture Organization of the United Nations 2005.

Western Europe averages are higher and increased at a greater rate than the world's overall, and industrialized countries as an aggregate had a slightly higher average than Western Europe, but with approximately the same rate of increase as Western Europe. The supply per capita per year of industrialized countries increased from 58 kg in 1961 to 93.3 kg in 2002, and the meat-supplied calories per capita per day during the same time increased from 255.4 to 387.8.

Australia, New Zealand, and United States, all home to livestock production and historically part of the global meat economy, are included in the industrialized countries aggregate, and this accounts for the slightly higher average than that of Western Europe alone (figure 1). From 1961 to 2002, Australia's very high supply per capita per year ranged from 103.9 kg to 108.8 kg; New Zealand's was very high, yet stable, ranging from 107.4 kg to 106.7 kg; the United States' 1961 average was not as high initially, but ended with the highest average of all, increasing from a supply per capita per year of 88.7 kg to 124.1 kg (Food and Agriculture Organization of the United Nations 2005).

Patterns of the global meat economy are also found in the aggregate of Latin America and the Caribbean. The supply per capita per year from 1961

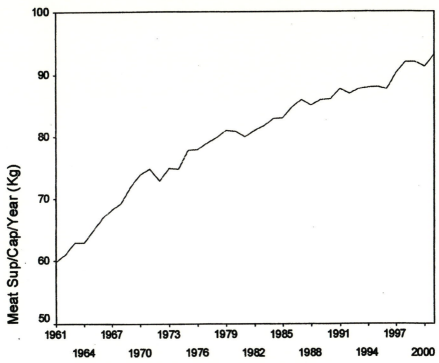

Figure 1. Industrialized Countries: Meat Supply Per Capita Per Year
Source: Food and Agriculture Organization of the United Nations 2004

to 2002 is higher than the world average and lower than that of both Western Europe and of industrialized countries, yet there are Latin American countries with averages as high as those found in the aggregate of industrialized countries. The Latin American supply per capita per year increased from 33.8 kg to 61.2 kg, with the livestock intensive Argentina, Paraguay, and Uruguay all being clear outliers. From 1961 to 2002, the supply per capita per year of Argentina ranged from 102.1 kg to 96.4 kg; Paraguay from 71.9 kg to 70.3 kg; and Uruguay from 107.8 kg to 77.7 kg (Food and Agriculture Organization of the United Nations 2005).

During this same time, in countries categorized by the United Nations as *low income*, there is dramatically less meat consumption. These countries historically have had neither the wealth nor the resources to participate in a global meat economy, either as consumers or as livestock producers, or in some cases, there are deeply entrenched cultural restrictions or

prohibitions against meat-eating. For example, Bangladesh has extremely low averages, from 3.2 kg to 3.1 kg, and similarly India, from 3.7 kg to 5.2 kg. Cambodia and Indonesia have low averages, but clear increases, with the former increasing from 4.9 kg to 13.9 kg, and the latter increasing from 3.5 kg to 8.2 kg. Gambia, Nigeria, and Rwanda provide additional examples of patterns of meat consumption in countries on the periphery of the global meat economy: Gambia decreased from 10.6 kg to 5.2 kg; Nigeria was low and fairly stable from 7.9 kg to 8.6 kg; and Rwanda ranged from 4 kg to 4.4 kg (Food and Agriculture Organization of the United Nations 2005).

EXPLAINING INCREASES

Historically and prehistorically, animal-based foods have been highly valued for their concentrated nutritional content. The extent to which meat has been included in human diets has depended on various environmental pressures, including available natural resources, societal organization, and population size. With the emergence of agrarian societies in at least seven independent centers globally (Smith 1998), humans ate less meat and more plants, and had less nutritional diversity in their diets. For centuries, most of the population in these agrarian societies received almost all of their calories from grains and other starchy staples, while a small elite portion of the population received a more diverse diet that included a high percentage of meats and other animal-based foods.

From a convergence of resources and social organization, a set of core countries emerged that would position Europe to control much of the world's wealth, technology of production, and scientific knowledge (Wallerstein 1979). As these core countries modernized and industrialized and moved from monarchies to democracies, the overall standard of living increased for much of the population in these countries. By the nineteenth century, areas colonized by core countries provided the much needed resource of land for livestock production and were incorporated into the transnational meat economy. These semi-peripheral areas and countries, while not having the wealth or economic control of core countries, did participate in the consumption of goods produced for a global market generated by core countries. Consumption of meat as wealth and health was overwhelming supported ideologically and economically by national political and health authorities as a global economy emerged and developed. Those countries on the extreme periphery of the world-system, although not economically or environmentally capable of sustaining a meat economy, were encouraged to increase their meat consumption for the sake of their population's health. During the middle and latter part of the twentieth century, theories of modernization were used to convince periphery countries to adopt the culture and consumption patterns of the most developed and core countries, resulting in increases in meat consumption even in countries that could not participate, as a resource or as a consumer, in a relatively expensive global meat economy.

Challenging the ideology of early modernization theories, there has been debate among scientists from various fields regarding the necessity of animal-based food in human diets. While some continue to argue that increased consumption of animal-based foods is necessary for positive micronutrient status and cognitive functioning, as well human and national development in general (Black 2003; Demment, Young and Sensenig 2003; Murphy and Allen 2003), others assert that diets based on plant foods can best prevent nutrient deficiencies and chronic health problems, and that vegetarian cultures and their diets do not equate with cognitive impairment and national underdevelopment (Hu 2003; Pimentel and Pimentel 2003; Sabate 2003). Similarly, while anthopometrists note a positive relationship between consumption of animal-based foods and increased height, a trend that has been noted repeatedly in developed and developing countries (Zemel, Eveleth and Johnston 1999), many researchers point out that non animal-based dietary alternatives and diversified plant based diets can supply the same nutrients as animal-based foods (Grigg 1993; Milton 2003).

MEAT CONSUMPTION AND ANIMAL PROTECTION

Regardless of the various ideologies, arguments, and debates surrounding the perceived nutritional necessities and advantages or disadvantages of meat in human diets, the very clear trend has been increased consumption of meat correlated with increases in industrialization and modernization. The explanation suggested in world-systems theories is that core countries led the way in increased levels of meat consumption, with access to meat became democratized and expanding with global economic systems. On the other hand, further explanation is offered through an examination of world-level culture, in which the consumption of meat, with its symbolic, economic, and nutritional values, has been part of the ideology of progress that promotes improvement and advancement in the human society. World-level culture, however, also presents the ideal society as committed to the alleviation of pain and suffering, as well as beneficent mastery of the natural world. The tension between these two ideological threads of meat consumption and of humane treatment is just beginning to be codified into world-level culture, as the constraints of resources, population, and extended rights converge in the twenty-first century.

Theories of economic development can help explain the increase in consumption of animal-based foods, and meat in particular, in that meat has been and continues to be highly valued. These same theories, however, cannot as completely explain the concurrent emergence of animal advocacy, initially in core countries, then later in other countries as they increase their economic status. Theories of world society and world-level culture can help explain both the democratization of meat consumption and the concurrent rise of animal protection in core countries, as well as the expansion of both, as countries strive to become global citizens. Similarly, theories that examine world-level culture can help explain the roles and influence of both the nation state and INGOs in animal protection. Informed by a synthesis of propositions from world-systems theories and theories of world society and its culture, those concerned with the topics at hand can achieve a clearer understanding of the most pervasive economic, cultural, and social aspect of human-animal relations—that of human consumption of other animals for food purposes.

Chapter Four

Animal Protection and the Nation-State

Currently, most societies in developed regions of the world are comfortable with killing animals for food purposes, as long as the animals are protected from suffering or pain. Many contemporary philosophers and legal scholars argue that animals should be protected based on their *inherent value* as individuals, rather than on their pain and suffering or on their status as human property. Although this once radical position of inherent value is becoming institutionalized and codified, most animal protection laws continue to be based on reducing the pain and suffering of animals destined to become human food, with governmental regulation and inspection being the normal methods of control.

Although religions and cultural systems have historically regulated the selection, preparation, and slaughter of animals for food purposes, they did not typically advocate or administer the protection of animals as individuals in any formal manner. The emergence of the nation-state as a political entity brought with it the formal protection of animals as individuals deserving of humane treatment and protection. The cruelty of animal baiting and issues of sanitation were sometimes the targets of early state-sponsored animal protection, but the state quickly took on and expanded the role of protector of animals used for food purposes. The explicit protection of the health and well-being of animals as individual living beings was a primary function of the state's involvement in animal protection, a role not formalized previously.

Government regulation of human use of animals increased since the nineteenth century, most clearly becoming the responsibility of the nation-state during the twentieth century, with the nation-state becoming the regulator and enforcer of all relations between humans and animals. The state has become the protector of animals, with the intention that animals be treated humanely and are subject to as little suffering as possible, as well as kept in conditions that do not compromise the health of either the animals or the consumers. This process of regulation by the nation-state started with those core countries home to epistemic communities that generated definitions of progress that included humane treatment of animals and extension of rights to animals as individuals.

In this chapter, early religious regulation of animal slaughter is first discussed, followed by a section that examines the nation-state's emerging role in animal protection. Attention is given to the emergence both of animal protection among elites in developed countries and of the nation-state's assumption of the role of animal protection as part of larger ideological project of improvement through humane social practices. With earlier religious regulation of slaughter and other interactions between humans and other animals, the concern had been for the effect on human souls. Animal protection as implemented by the nation-state, however, was grounded in the assumption that animals were individuals that could suffer and feel pain, and that reduction of this pain and suffering would contribute to the greater social good.

Contributing to an understanding of world-level culture and animal protection, this chapter examines the relationship between the early nineteenth century emergence of the state as animal protector and the early animal advocates from the aristocracy and urban elite who prompted that emergence. These elites and the legislation they proposed, as well as the state's assumption of the role of protector, are grounded in the idea of progress developed in the eighteenth and nineteenth centuries. This idea of progress included such propositions as the advancement of knowledge and technology, the elimination of ignorance generated by superstition and religions, the practice of justice and pity, and overcoming human cruelty and violence though improving both social conditions and governments. Nation-states, shaped by world-level culture, accepted and supported the assumption that animal protection is a function of the ideal nation-state.

Finally, this chapter discusses how animal protection by the nation-state has been fully institutionalized, with the pain and suffering of animals used for human food, the health of both the consumed and the consumer, and the sustainability of resources all being given high priority in creation of current public policy. This institutionalization and codifying of animal protection has occurred over the past two centuries, not because of grassroots mobilization or emergence of new social movements, but rather as a consequence of the expansion of a world-level cultural expectation regarding the role of the nation-state.

EARLY REGULATION OF ANIMAL SLAUGHTER

In Hinduism, killing of an animal has historically been considered murder, although both animals and humans were arranged in a hierarchy that assigned more significance to the killing of a cow or Brahman than, for example, a dog or an *untouchable*. As with Hinduism, Buddhism teaches the belief in rebirth of the soul in both human and animal form. Buddha taught that it was a sin to kill any living creature and advocated friendliness towards all living things (Bukkyo Dendo Kyokai 1978). Killing of animals for food purposes has not been supported in Hinduism and Buddhism, with the exception of the practice of animal sacrifice abandoned very early in both traditions. Regulation in this religious context was enforced by individuals practicing nonviolence, such as the application of the Buddhist doctrine of *ahisma* by Asoka, Emperor of India, in which he condemned royal hunts and the slaughter of animals during his rule in the third century BC (Asoka [259 BC]1958; Sanghavarman 1993).

Both Jainism and Manicheans commanded that followers practice radical nonviolence based on respect for the individual life of each creature. The Jains' supreme vow was and is *not to kill*, with even insects being included in this command (Laidlaw 1995). Manicheans, followers of the third century Mani of Persia, were also forbidden to kill any living thing, although this was truly only practiced by an orthodox core group and not the secularized followers (Spencer 1996). Although neither Jainism nor Manicheanism regulated the killing of animals by the majority of the population, both traditions exerted control over a very small percentage of the population through the command of universally applied nonviolence. Interestingly, this command was not based on the reduction of suffering, but rather on a belief in the inherent value of each individual creature, a position shared by the twentieth century radical animal rights movement.

Within the Abramic traditions, both Judaism and Islam codified the killing of animals for food, including strict guidelines for both the adherents' diet and related animal slaughter. For the most part, Christian doctrine did and does not expect adherents to comply to Jewish or any other dietary laws, with the exception of some sects and cults, such as modern Seventh Day Adventists. *Kashrut*, the Jewish dietary code, allows the slaughter and consumption of animals, even though vegetarianism is presented in Genesis as the ideal diet and behavior for humans. In Genesis, Noah is presented as the initiator of meat-eating, with divine permission granted with the provision that humans will not bite into living animals nor consume their blood. The Noachic laws include prohibitions against hunting, and command humans to eat only meat chosen from flocks and properly sacrificed (Dresner, Siegel and Pollock 1982). Although *kashrut* has been traditionally interpreted by rabbis as having both the intention of controlling the appetite for meat and the purpose of enforcing a sensitivity to animal life, the practiced emphasis has been on following codes for slaughter and celebration (Cooper 1993). Regulation of slaughter is clearly important, and sensitivity to the sacrificed animal is implied according to rabbinic interpretations, but the focus is on human violation of laws and controlling lust, rather than on the well-being and individual suffering of the sacrificial animal. Interestingly, some of the early animal protection legislation enacted by modern states was in direct response to the methods of slaughter practiced by Jewish communities in nineteenth century Europe, methods strictly codified in *kashrut*. This tension continues, as seen in the 2002 banning, in some cases continuations of bans, of kosher food production by at least five European countries on the grounds of animal cruelty.

Similar to the Jewish *kashrut*, Islam provided strict codes for the slaughtering and consumption of animals. Only meat designated as *halal* was codified as acceptable for human consumption. The flesh of animals that are both "clean" and properly slaughtered are considered *halal*, with the flesh of scavengers strictly prohibited (Hussaini 1993; Institute of Islamic Jurisprudence of UK 1997). During slaughter, which is considered a ritual act, a Muslim must consecrate the act of killing through pronouncing specified words and cutting the animal's throat with "mercifully quick strokes." If an animal was killed during a hunt, the meat is considered *halal* only if consecrating words were spoken during the kill. Overall, the regulatory emphasis has and continues to be on whether or not the animal was "clean" and consecrated, rather than on protection of the individual animal. Islamic tradition has associated meat-eating positively with religiosity, and exceptions to this behavior, such as two early female Sufi saints' refusal to eat meat, were persecuted or questioned (Smith 1978; Smith 2001). As with Judaism's *kashrut* practices, Islam's practice of *halal* has been questioned and challenged in modern Europe. Contemporary legislation has been directed specifically at prohibiting *halal* methods of animal slaughter, with the intention being to protect the well-being or reduce the suffering of the slaughtered animal.

A few Christian sects, such as the Slavic Bogomils, the eleventh century Cathars, and contemporary Seventh Day Adventists (Spencer 1996), have been concerned with creating doctrine regulating or prohibiting consumption of meat. However, there are no Christian dietary codes, or rules concerning the slaughter and treatment of animals used as food. The few syncretic Christian pagan or heretical groups that strictly prohibited the killing and eating of animals, did so based on their abhorrence of the corporeal, rather than on the premise that animals should be protected (Grant 1961; Lupieri 2002; McGinn, Meyendorff and Leclercq 1985). Similarly, Christian saints, including Jerome, Benedict of Nursia, Francis of Assisi, Erasmus, and Thomas More, all believed that eating animals led to being controlled by carnal desires and appetites. Again, the concern was not for any recognized inherent value of the animal nor for protection of the animal, but was rather an objection on ascetic grounds (Walters and Portmess 2001). Historically, the Christian idea of dominion defined animals in terms of serving and feeding humanity, rather than the very recent focus, expressed in some Christian theology, on compassionate stewardship of the earth (Scully 2002). Historically or presently, neither dietary and slaughter codes, nor the notion of animal protection have been essential to Christian doctrine, although ideas of compassion and justice as they relate to human-animal relations have been utilized by a few individual Christians involved in animal advocacy.

Codified regulation of animal slaughter and meat consumption is most clearly seen in the Abramic tradition, specifically Judaism and Islam, but is directed at dietary control, definitions of clean (pure) and unclean (impure), and control of bloodlust, rather than at protecting the animal itself as an individual or at imbuing humans with qualities of mercy. With the compartmentalization of religion taking place as modern states developed and expanded, what religious regulation of food animals did exist was clearly eclipsed by state regulation and state population interests. By the nineteenth century, nation-states had clearly ascended to power in political, social, and economic spheres, and had begun institutionalizing and enforcing the protection of animals on the grounds of preserving the well-being and reducing any suffering experienced by the individual animal destined for human consumption.

EARLY ANIMAL PROTECTION LEGISLATION

Britain

In 1822 under George IV, England enacted the first animal protection legislation by parliamentary procedure, known commonly as Martin's Act and officially entitled An Act to Prevent the Cruel and Improper Treatment of Cattle. It was sponsored by Richard Martin, MP, a native Irish estate owner educated at Cambridge (Lynam 1975). John Lawrence, a gentleman-farmer who had written extensively on the *jus animalium*, and Thomas Erskine, former Lord Chancellor of the House of Lords, had previously failed to pass animal protection legislation and assisted Martin in this first success in a series of related efforts. All were influenced by a community of friends and peers that included Jeremy Bentham and David Hume, as well as others who reconceptualized the status of non-humans.

These initial animal protection legislators worked towards installing the state as protector of animals, on the grounds that it was an essential, specific element of the general idea of humane treatment, which included a range of other social issues such as capital punishment, treatment of prisoners, child abuse, and equal access to legal aid. Richard Martin, born into a Roman Catholic family of Dublin, but educated as a Protestant in England, was a political independent who supported both the Union with Great Britain and Catholic Emancipation.

As an MP and a citizen at large, Martin was considered a comical, yet effective speaker, had a reputation as both a duelist and a humanitarian, and in general was considered a dependable source of entertainment (Fairholme and Pain 1924). Two days after the passage of the Treatment of Cattle Act in 1822, Martin personally and successfully applied the law to two men beating horses in the market at Smithfield. He regularly patrolled the streets of London in search of acts of cruelty towards animals, but successful convictions occurred only against "improper treatment of horses, mares, geldings, mules, asses, cows, heifers, steers, oxen, sheep, and other cattle" as stated in law. Known for his extreme, relentless pursuit of offenders, as well as for paying the fines for violators expressing remorse, Martin was a key figure in shaping public opinion in favor of animal protection, and was instrumental in the formation of the Society for the Prevention of Cruelty to Animals (Farrell 2004; Lynam 1975).

Several early English attempts at organizations that promoted animal protection, such as the Society for the Suppression of Vice (1802) and the Society for Preventing Wanton Cruelty to Animals (1809), were temporary and met only a few times. In 1824, two years after the enactment of Martin's Law, the Society for the Prevention of Cruelty to Animals was formed and although attended by Martin, it was initially headed by Thomas Fowell Buxton, active in anti-slavery campaigns and other reform efforts, and Reverend Arthur Broome, who is described as the society's founder. Twenty-one people, all men, are noted in the SPCA's first minutes, including three clergymen and five members of Parliament (Brown 1974; Fairholme and Pain 1924; Moss 1961). Buxton was a Dorset MP, described as philanthropist and parliamentary reformer, who had married into a prominent Quaker family. He was an executive member of the ecumenical London City Mission, a organization that engaged in missionary work with cab drivers (May 1995). Buxton also introduced motions in Parliament for and published works on the abolishment of slavery (Buxton [1839]1968; Mottram 1946), and actively supported reform of both the penal system and children's educational system (Buxton 1818; Buxton 1984).

Continental Europe

Although individual advocates began calling for improved treatment of animals in the late 1700s, organized animal protection emerged in German states in the 1830s, with membership consisting of middle-class clergy, civil servants, policemen, town councilmen, physicians, teachers, and lawyers. Over the next few decades, German animal protection societies called for the improved transport of animals, teaching animal protection in schools, and the creation of animal protection laws (Judd 2003). In 1860, the first international animal protection congress was held in Dresden (Niven 1967), and by 1871, all German states except the city-state of Lübreck had enacted legislation or ordinances against animal cruelty in public. Interestingly, animal protection groups began directed efforts at livestock protection around this time, when slaughter was being removed from the public eye and the mass production of meat was escalating. In Berlin, the number of slaughtered animals would rise from 731,326 in 1871 to 1,614,791 in 1900 (Berlin 1871-1919). Reformers in German states and other European states worked for the establishment of public slaughterhouses that would be licensed and regulated by municipalities and the state (Brantz 2002).

Historically, German culture had philosophically and politically supported animal protection at least since the eighteenth century. Immanuel Kant had argued in favor of animal protection in 1785, when he publicly supported animal protection. He grounded his argument in the belief that an individual who abused animals would be led into similar abuses towards other humans, especially those humans least capable of defending themselves (Sorabji 1993). This argument continued to gather support in Germany during the nineteenth century. In their petition to the German Reichstag in 1886 calling for national legislation on humane slaughter, the National Association of Animal Protection Societies criticized the "deplorable state of affairs surrounding the method of slaughtering, the role of the butcher, and finally the demoralizing effect that the sight of this albeit necessary killing of livestock must have, particularly on the youth" (Brantz 2002:167).

In Switzerland, animal protection legislation aimed at defining humane slaughter and the reduction of animal suffering occurred relatively early in 1874, when Swiss national law required that animals be rendered insensible before slaughter. Although public agitation against *shechita* (Jewish kosher butchery practices) would escalate and converge with anti-Semitic rhetoric during the late nineteenth century (Kulling 1977), it is important to note that the Swiss government and parliament were against defining *shechita* as an illegal, inhumane practice. During the 1880s, the Swiss Society for the Protection of Animals officially began campaigning against *shechita* and utilized the Swiss constitution's provision for public initiative and referendum. In 1893, the Swiss electorate voted in favor of including *shechita* as an illegal, inhumane method of slaughter (Steinberg and Guggenheim-Grünberg 1966). The prohibition of kosher butchery practices, as codified in humane slaughter laws, has continued uninterrupted in Switzerland to the present day.

In southern European countries, there was no real position taken by states on animal protection nor related legislation in the nineteenth century. This could be due to the decidedly Catholic presence, and thus a Thomist approach to non-human animals, or perhaps a different interpretation of the biblical concept of *dominion* from that of the more Protestant north. The lower economic status of southern Europe has also been suggested as a possible cause for this difference, in that lower economic status might prevent a population from the spending of emotional, temporal, or economic resources on the protection of non-humans.

North American

With the exception of the Puritans, who included provisions against cruelty towards animals in transit in their 1641 legal code The Body of Liberties, written by the English lawyer Nathanial Ward earlier accused of heresy, legislation protecting animals was not enacted in the Americas until well into the nineteenth century. In the late nineteenth century, in response to concerns over the conditions of cattle cars, and the cruelty and diseases related to this method of rail transport, the Twenty-Eight Hour Law was passed by the United States Congress in 1873. Cattle traveled across the United States without food or water for a long as five days, then were slid into holding pens where feed, if any, was dumped straight into the contaminated mud. Frequently, smaller animals such as calves, sheep, and swine, would be crowded under adult cattle in rail cars, with this method prevailing across the United States (United States Department of Agriculture 1978).

In general, the profile of late nineteenth century United States advocates of animal protection was highly educated, higher socio-economic status, extensive national and international travel, some social exposure to members of the United States abolitionist movement, some political affiliations with religious organizations, but above all, dedicated to the idea of making society increasingly humane. True to much of United States social change, influential individuals in the early animal protection movement, although not promoting animal protection on religious grounds, did nurture associations with some pastors willing to use the pulpit to endorse animal protection as correct and humane action. Similarly, these influential individuals in the animal protection movement addressed audiences outside of religious services, in assemblies sponsored by religious organizations, such as the Episcopalian or Unitarian Churches.

Although many religious groups and individuals, such as the Quakers or the Puritans, did preach compassion towards animals, they did not organize or spearhead the animal protection movement. Organized efforts at animal protection occurred with the development of principles of *humane treatment* and ideas of progress in epistemic communities that were interested in civic and democratic life, rather than in promulgating religious values. As with leaders in current community organizing in the United States, and as exemplified in models of organizing proposed by Saul Alinsky and others, early advocates of animal protection saw religious groups not just as faith communities, but as existing networks that can be employed in the diffusion and propagation of positions on social issues.

Nineteenth century animal advocacy in the United States *did* have a connection to the abolitionist movement in a way that other issues, such as temperance, suffrage, or penal reform, did not. For animal protection to be presented to and accepted by the United States public in general, it was first necessary for slavery to be abolished, in that legislators, potential patrons, and citizens recognized that the public prioritizes human needs over the needs of non-humans . A few years after the ratification of the Thirteenth Amendment of the United States Constitution, a journalist in *Scribner's* acknowledged this relationship, noting that the emergence of animal protection "was first rendered possible by the liberation of the slave, because a reasonable people could not have listened to the claims of dumb animals while human beings, held in more ignoble bondage, were subjected to greater cruelty and added outrage" (Buel 1879).

In the decade following the abolition of slavery, not only did some abolitionists turn their attention to animal concerns, but animal protection organizations in the United States secured the first anti-cruelty legislation in their respective state legislatures. While abolitionists' works, such as *Queer Little People* (Stowe 1867) and *The Freedmen's Book* (Child [1865]1968), sought to teach humane treatment of animals through didactic literature written for children and liberated slaves, animal protection was championed in the political arena by wealthy citizens with both the social and economic capital to initiate and sustain the campaigns necessary to enact legislation.

Early animal protection in the United States was advocated on the premise that modern society should be humane, whether taught through children's books or delivered in political venues to adult audiences. While abolitionists and others who wrote for a juvenile audience, such as Anna Sewell and her immensely popular book *Black Beauty: the Autobiography of a Horse, Translated from the Original Equine* ([1877]1990), can be seen as disseminating ideas and values through mass education, Henry Bergh and George Angell are representative of the process of the state accepting the role of defining and regulating animal protection through legislation.

Both mass education and legislation aimed to make animal protection the societal norm, on the premise that it was humane, and modern, civilized societies should be humane. Although clearly claims were made asserting that to be humane was to be moral, those organizations and individuals involved in legislating animal protection in the United States did not equate being humane with being religious. Some advocates of animal protection did have very religious parents or parents involved in church politics, but animal protection legislation was not enacted as a religious measure.

Organized animal protection in the United States began in the 1860s in New York City, Boston, and Philadelphia, and spread across the nation over the next decade. Henry Bergh, member of an aristocratic New York shipbuilding family, formed the American Society for the Prevention of Cruelty to Animals in 1866 with the support of the New York legislature. In 1867, Caroline Earle White, daughter of a well-known Quaker slavery abolitionist, led the formation of the Pennsylvania Society for the Prevention of Cruelty to Animals, after visiting and corresponding with Bergh in New York and gaining extremely strong support from the wealthy elite of Philadelphia.

George Angell, Massachusetts lawyer, abolitionist, and son of a teacher, formed the Massachusetts Society for the Prevention of Cruelty to Animals in 1868, after interaction with Henry Bergh and Emily Appleton, a Bostonian who had already been corresponding with Bergh. All were influenced by existing networks and organizations in England, and continued to draw on the experience of these English groups as they formed similar organizations across the United States.

Henry Bergh had traveled throughout Europe and the Near East, and recorded instances of animal cruelty in his diaries as early as the 1840s (Steele 1942). Bergh became known not just for observing, but also for intervening in animal cruelty. In 1863, while serving as Secretary of the American Legation in the court of Czar Alexander II in St. Petersburg, Bergh ordered a peasant driver to stop beating a horse, an intervention he reportedly repeated many times, on many different roads in and outside of Russia (Harlow 1957). Returning from Russia in 1865, Bergh spent a few months in England, and very likely met Lord Harrowby, president of the Royal Society for the Prevention of Cruelty to Animals at a memorial service for Abraham Lincoln. Bergh attended the RSPCA's annual meeting and met with the society's officers (Royal Society for the Prevention of Cruelty to Animals 1872; 1888), and subsequently returned to New York with plans for a similar society in the United States.

In early 1866, Bergh announced his plans to form an animal protection society, and began mobilizing New York City's social elite. Although there was opposition from powerful streetcar and slaughterhouse interests in the New York Assembly, Bergh secured a charter of incorporation with the help of United States Senator Charles Folger. Shortly after, this newly chartered American Society for the Prevention of Cruelty to Animals was also granted power to enforce all animal protection laws in the state of New York (McCrea [1910]1969). On April 19, 1866, An Act to Better Prevent Cruelty to Animals was enacted as New York law, stating that "every person who shall, by his act or neglect, maliciously kill, maim, wound, injure, torture or cruelly beat any horse, mule, ox, cattle, sheep, or other animal belonging to himself or another, shall upon conviction, be adjudged guilty of a misdemeanor" and included a clause addressing abandonment of "worn out" or "unwanted" animals (Edmonds 1868). Bergh continued cultivating alliances with local and state politicians, including Republicans, Tammany Democrats, and New York City's Mayor Hoffman, and successfully gained support for the ASPCA (*New York Times* 1871), even though many of these organizations and individuals were financially involved in streetcar companies and slaughterhouses, as well as recreationally involved in pigeon shooting and fox hunting (Steele 1942).

The charter of the ASPCA provided for the cooperation of the police force of New York City, as well as empowering any citizen to cause an arrest by reporting acts of cruelty or neglect to a police officer, or by making a complaint before a magistrate (American Society for the Prevention of Cruelty to Animals 1866). Like his English counterpart, Richard Martin, Bergh created a very high and dramatic profile for animal protection law by personally admonishing individuals engaged in any mistreatment of animals in the streets of New York City or elsewhere. Establishments and industries that involved horses or cattle also experienced unfavorable and heightened public profiles. Bergh would select an issue, such as slaughterhouse cruelty, the swill milk producers that were located adjacent to distilleries, or street trolley horse abuse, and focus attention on it for as long as it took to get the newspapers and public engaged, outraged, or disgusted.

As in Europe, Jewish *shehitah* was also scrutinized, and Bergh contacted New York rabbis and circulated a related letter to kosher slaughterers asking whether or not animals might first be rendered unconscious before being slit, hoisted by one leg, and bled to death. The resistance and negative response he received from rabbis led Bergh to exempt Jewish slaughter from all proposals he made regarding regulations, although he would continue to voice his dislike for *shehitah* whenever he was questioned on the topic (Unti 2002).

New York newspapers and magazines reported regularly on Bergh, the ASPCA, and the establishments and conditions exposed. *Frank Leslie's, New York Times, New York Herald*, and other publications printed exposés, descriptions, events, schedules, and editorials that fanned public interest. Weekly, sometimes daily, reports revealed and described such scenes as swill milk cows being treated cruelly and producing poisonous milk, hogs being hoisted in the air by one leg and dropped into boiling water, chickens being plucked alive, turtles oozing blood in the market, and horses being worked to death then converted to glue and cheap hide (Unti 2002). Related arrests, counted as victories by the ASPCA and sympathizers, and editorials were also printed frequently and regularly.

Although not as flamboyant nor aristocratic as Bergh, George Angell founded the Massachusetts Society for the Prevention of Cruelty to Animals in 1868 using a similar membership base in Boston, promoting direct and aggressive involvement with legislators, and encouraging public exposure to animal related issues. Angell's mother was a schoolteacher, and his father, who died in Angell's toddler years, was a Baptist minister. After graduating from Dartmouth University in 1846, Angell taught in the Boston public schools and attended Harvard Law School until 1851, when he was admitted to the bar and became a partner of the Massachusetts abolitionist Samuel Sewell (Angell 1884). As with Bergh and the ASPCA in New York, Angell enjoyed regular exposure in newspapers and magazines in Boston, as well as access to a prominent publishing house through Emily Appleton, one of Angell's co-organizers and wife of William Appleton (American Society for the Prevention of Cruelty to Animals 1905). These circumstances facilitated Angell's eventual realization of his goal of a broad-based public education initiative regarding the treatment of animals.

Angell and the MSPCA began the first regular animal protection publication, *Our Dumb Animals*, in 1868, and distributed 200,000 copies door to door with the help of the Boston police force, who continued this service for several years (Hansen-Lappen 1993). Years later, William Stillman of the American Humane Association recalled that Angell personally sent the magazine to every doctor, lawyer, and clergyman in Massachusetts because he believed that they were the most likely to be consulted when people executed their wills (American Humane Association 1920). The magazine was designed to attract the support of the public, and included news, narratives of both humane intervention and virtuous animals, and commentary on all things related to animal protection. An interesting example is a supportive review and discussion of Julia Eastman's juvenile book *Striking for the Right*, in which a kindness club is formed by children in a Massachusetts town with the assistance of their teacher. In Eastman's book, the teacher presents the children's cause in the adult venues, openly contradicting the local pastor's position on animal rights, confronting abusive teamsters, and condemning the treatment of cattle. Through the educational efforts of the children and the teacher, the townspeople abandon their cruel treatment of animals (Eastman 1872; Massachusetts Society for the Prevention of Cruelty to Animals 1873).

As with the state of New York and the ASPCA, the Massachusetts legislature had approved the 1868 charter of MSPCA and its right to enforce laws related to animal cruelty. Angell and the MSPCA dedicated much of their efforts towards educating and creating legislation for the humane treatment of horses and animals destined for slaughter. In 1872, Angell began a supplemental to *Our Dumb Animals* entitled "Cattle Transportation" that presented public health issues framed in the context of animal protection issues, including discussions of the effect of cruelty on the animals' emotional state and consequently on the quality of meat, and the effects of animals witnessing the death of other animals (Angell 1872). As with Bergh and the ASPCA, Angell and the MSPCA investigated, discussed, and then exempted Jewish ritual slaughter from their proposals for regulation and reform (Angell 1870; Guinzburg 1870).

At the national level, the MSPCA's efforts and Angell's publications were extremely important in the transformation of animal slaughter into an issue on the national legislative agenda and the passing of the federal Twenty-Eight Hour Law of 1873. Similarly, the MSPCA's related work with legislators was extremely important in defining the state's role in regulating cattle that would be codified in the federal government's Food and Drugs Act of 1906 (Young 1989). Throughout the 1870s and 1880s, Angell personally helped organize humane societies in Illinois, Wisconsin, Connecticut, and Washington, DC (Angell 1884). Along with others, such as Henry Bergh, Angell imported ideas and values about animal protection into all areas of the United States through publication and distribution of educational materials, and targeted campaigning at individuals and groups that had political and economic power in their communities.

By the 1870s, the national collaborative efforts of humane societies were focused on a campaign to end the suffering of animals destined for slaughter, in particular their sufferings during transit. The work of the ASPCA and the MSCPA in the 1860s was directly responsible for constructing animal protection as a national issue, and for the subsequent federal laws enacted beginning with the 1873 Twenty-Eight Hour Law, which regulated the amount of time and the traveling environment of cattle and all livestock in transit to and from the stockyards and slaughterhouses.

In the United States, animal protection was organized and institutionalized by individuals and groups with social, cultural, and economic capital. English animal protection organizations and legislation were observed and imported by United States citizens, who quickly established and modified the English models as needed. Public support was gathered through distribution of adult and juvenile literature, including newsletters and novels, as well as through supportive journalists in magazines and newspapers. Although the idea of humane treatment was premised on the necessity of moral action, it was not explicitly promoted as a condition of human spiritual salvation or religious doctrine. The suffering and virtuous animal was the prevailing image presented in writing, graphics, and speech by supporters of animal protection, with the animal being seen as a individual that could experience both pain and suffering in a way similar to humans. Through mass education and legislation, humane treatment of animals could be taught and enforced as a national program, with the nation-state, at both the state and federal levels, being seen as responsible for regulating treatment of animals. By the end of the nineteenth century, animal protection had clearly become the responsibility of the nation-state.

A twist remains, in that the suffering and feelings of animals were a primary symbolic tool used to build public support for humane treatment, yet there was no effort to prevent or reduce the slaughter or death of animals. Both the death and the consumption of turtles, fish, cattle, horses, chickens and all animals on the menu were accepted without question by animal protectionists and the overwhelming majority, but cruelty and suffering were not to be permitted in a civilized society that recognized that all animals could feel and were to some extent sentient. Although the *inherent value* argument, strongly supported and developed during the twentieth century, was implicitly present in the nineteenth century belief that animals were individuals who could feel and were aware of their own existence, inherent value did not yet extend to equating the value of animal life to the value of human life.

In a related example of animal protectionist reasoning, both Bergh and Angell proposed hippophagy as helping alleviate cattle transportation cruelties and as a benefit to the horses themselves, and promoted related discussions in public (Bowditch 1868; Massachusetts Society for the Prevention of Cruelty to Animals 1868; 1874; *New York Times* 1875). According to this proposal, if a popular taste for horse flesh could be cultivated in the United States, old, weak, or disabled horses could be spared the hardship of labor, and they would not need to be transported as did cattle, sheep, and hogs. Animals were to be protected by the state from pain and suffering, were anthropomorphized in literature and graphics, and were beginning to be constructed as individuals with rights, but no one was suggesting that the human slaughter and consumption of animals should end. Success was measured not in animal life spared, but rather in improved cattle cars, humane methods of slaughter, and demonstrations of kindness.

As in much of Britain and northern Europe, the nation-state in the United States became the administrator of animal protection, forcing economic and political entities to spend the resources necessary to alleviate the pain and suffering of animals. The general public came to support the premises and conditions of animal protection through educational initiatives that both anthropomorphized animals and presented them as potential public health risks. Cruelty and disease were constructed as scientifically inseparable, while kindness and sanitation were presented as twin virtues characteristic of modern, civilized societies. The first federal law related to animal protection, the Twenty-Eight Hour Law, was passed in 1873 and marked the clear beginning of the state's role as permanent administrator of animal protection. This law addressed transport of animals, but the meat-producing industry was slow in responding to the law. By 1900, technological and organizational innovations in the slaughter and transport of livestock made the Twenty-Eight Hour Law, which required improved feeding, watering, and care of cattle and other animals in transit, very rarely applicable for any of the animals being raised and processed in the new agricultural-industrial complex.

The End of the Nineteenth Century

By the end of the nineteenth century, the nation-state in most of northern Europe, Britain, the United States, and Canada had assumed the responsibility of administrating and enforcing animal protection. There were some notable differences among different regions or countries, including enactment dates of the first laws, application of laws, and penalties for violators. For example, in Germany, Switzerland, and some Scandinavian countries, laws defining humane methods of slaughter were universally enforced, leading to accusations of anti-Semitism and violation of religious freedoms. In Britain, the United States, and Canada, exemption from humane slaughter laws and other animal protection laws was and continues to be granted to both kosher and *halal* slaughterhouses, albeit at the organized protest of many animal advocates.

Other European countries, such as France, Spain, and Italy, add to the differences among regions and countries at the end of the nineteenth century. France had a humane society by 1845, modeled on the British RSPCA, yet at the same time, had no animal protection legislation and practiced nationally funded vivisection at universities and medical schools throughout the nineteenth century. In Spain, each region created different laws and levels of enforcement regarding the treatment of animals, and there continues to be no clear national animal protection legislation of any type. In Italy, the political activist Guisseppe Garibaldi founded the first animal protection society in Italy, *Ente Nazionale Protezione Animali*, in 1871. Overall, Italy has moved towards national administration of animal protection, although there seems to have existed cultural habits supportive of humane treatment of animals previous to any legislation.

ANIMAL PROTECTION IN THE TWENTIETH CENTURY

In the twentieth century, the state in developed countries has fully assumed the role of administrating animal protection. Building on over a hundred years of precedence, animal welfare legislation in the United Kingdom is created and changed only by Parliament, although members of Parliament are pressured by individuals and organizations to implement changes. With animals used for food purposes, animal protection laws affect livestock owners, hauliers, auctioneers, slaughterhouse operators, and local authorities. These groups are monitored both by state agencies, such as the Ministry of Agriculture, Fisheries, and Food, by local authority inspectors and police, and by animal welfare groups, including the Royal Society for the Prevention of Cruelty to Animals. Current legislation defines the minimum standards considered necessary to protect the welfare of animals used for food purposes, as well as penalties for individuals and groups that cause "unnecessary suffering" by any activity or neglect (Radford 2001).

The twentieth century profile of United Kingdom animal welfare is can be sketched using The Protection of Animals Act 1911, Agriculture (Miscellaneous Provisions) Act 1968, the Welfare of Livestock Regulations 1994, the Welfare of Livestock (Amendment) Regulations 1998, and Welfare of Farmed Animals (England) Regulations 2000. The Protection of Animals Act 1911 contains the general law relating to cruelty to animals, including the prohibition against causing them unnecessary suffering. The welfare of all farmed "livestock" on "agricultural land" is further protected by the Agriculture (Miscellaneous Provisions) Act 1968, which makes it an offense to cause or allow unnecessary pain or unnecessary distress. The Welfare of Livestock Regulations 1994 and the Welfare of Livestock (Amendment) Regulations 1998 reformed earlier legislation with a primary intent being the reduction of pain and distress, but was replaced by in 2000 by The Welfare of Farmed Animals (England) Regulations 2000 (S.I. 2000 No. 1870) and a series of related legislation, which implemented EU Council Directive 98/58/EC into English, Scottish, Welsh, and Northern Irish law. This directive came out of the 1998 European Convention for the Protection of Animals Kept for Farming Purposes, and orders the European Union community of member states to enact the principles of the Convention. These principles include providing for the physiological and ethological needs of all farm animals, uniform application of related rules regarding rearing of livestock, adherence to welfare requirements, and uniform application of common minimum standards for the protection of animals, all of which should contribute to ensuring the rational development of production and the elimination of distortions of competition.

Serving as a receptor site for world-level cultural elements (Frank, Hironaka and Schofer 2000), the Department for Environment, Food, and Rural Affairs was created in June 2001, merging the Ministry of Agriculture, Fisheries, and Food and the Department of the Environment, Transport, and the Regions. DEFRA not only assumed the roles previously enacted by MAFF and DETR, but also implemented an organizational agenda and structure that formalized distribution channels of policy shaped by world-level culture. One of DEFRA's priorities has been reforming animal legislation in the United Kingdom so that it reflects European Union legislation, as well as United Nations policy on flora, fauna, and sustainable development (Barling, Lang and Caraher 2002; British Veterinary Association 2004).

Clearly situated in an international context, the stated primary functions of DEFRA include creation of European Union and global policy. This trend can be noted in earlier United Kingdom implementation of European Union policy, such as the United Kingdom's 1995 enactment of the Welfare of Animals (Slaughter or Killing) Regulations in direct response to EU Directive 93/119/EC issued in 1993 on the protection of animals at the time of slaughter or killing. In both cases, with the European Union as one primary generator of world-level culture and the United Kingdom as a receptor and distribution site of world-level cultural elements, codified values require that animals must not be subjected to avoidable excitement, pain or suffering before or during slaughter, and must be stunned before slaughter so that they are unconscious and unable to feel pain.

In general, animal protection legislation in European Union member contries have followed a path similar to that of the United Kingdom, with most European countries enacting increasingly strict legislation regarding moment of death, as well as an increasingly scientific definition of pain, suffering, and animal awareness. Although national humane slaughter legislation was enacted in several European countries beginning in 1874 with Switzerland, followed by the Netherlands, Norway, Scotland, Germany, Ireland, England, Finland, Sweden, and Denmark by 1953, the values reflected in animal protection are not national in origin. This legislation is not nationally bound in its values or goals, but reflects a global trend towards the strengthening of a world-level culture that asserts the protection of animals as a primary value and goal, to be reinforced and dispersed through such political entities as the nation-state. Other core countries have followed this trend, with countries and regions that have more recently been integrated into global socio-economic systems also showing signs of moving towards codifying animal protection.

Development of national animal protection legislation in the United States and Canada has followed a pattern similar to that found in European legislation. North America and Europe had experienced a similar convergence of urban population growth, increased economic prosperity, increased meat consumption, and the ideology of progress. However, North American countries' position in the supply chain of the global meat economy created economic and political circumstances that distinguished them from European countries. This distinction is evident in the somewhat later development of national legislation in the United States when compared to countries in Europe or the United Kingdom. In the United States in 1873 and 1877, the Twenty-Eight Hour Law had been enacted and revised in direct response to documented cruelties against animals in transit, and a series of short statutes addressing humane methods of slaughter had been adopted by Congress from 1901 to 1907. Not only was this early legislation considered a dead letter and unenforceable, there was no subsequent animal transport or humane slaughter federal legislation for over half a century.

In 1955, when Senator Hubert Humphrey introduced the first federal humane slaughter bill ever presented to the Senate, the battle ensuing between political leaders and meat packers can be partially understood as a conflict between the values of an expanding world-level culture and the economic mandates of a national meat industry. Following several failed attempts, related bills were reintroduced (United States 1956), with humane slaughter legislation being supported by the American Humane Association, the Animal Welfare Institute, the National Farmers' Union, the Society for Animal Protective Legislation, and many other humane organizations and church groups.

The opposition to this humane slaughter legislation included the United States Department of Agriculture, the American Meat Institute, the Farm Bureau, the National Cattlemen's Association, the National Grange, and the Union of Orthodox Rabbis (Leavitt 1990). In 1958, the Humane Slaughter Bill, although somewhat weakened by the Case-Javitts Amendment that exempted kosher-killed animals from humane slaughter, was signed into law by President Eisenhower.

The Humane Methods of Slaughter Act initially covered those United States packing companies that sold meat to the federal government, about 80% of all United States plants, but was expanded in 1978 to include livestock at all plants in the United States. The 1978 amendment gave power to federal inspectors to stop processing lines and added the requirement that all meat imported into the United States must be from animals slaughtered in accord with the Humane Methods of Slaughter Act. The most recent federal legislation occurred in 2002 when President George Bush signed into law the Farm Security and Rural Investment Act (Public Law 107-171), which includes a resolution that the Humane Methods of Slaughter Act of 1958 should be fully enforced to prevent the needless suffering of animals, and enlists the Secretary of Agriculture to track violations and report the results and trends annually to Congress.

In some ways, the United States and the European Union, although clearly very different in political organization, are similar in that both can be seen as agents of a world-level culture that channels values and goals to member states. Animal protection is a value and goal of world-level culture, and nation-states adhering to the ideology of progress will accept implementation of animal protection as evidence both of advancement and of global status. A related process has been noted in explanations of the rise of national activities directed at protecting the environment. Global definitions of the nation-state during the twentieth century came to include environmental protection as a state responsibility, with the "blueprints" of nation-state environmentalism drawn at the world level, then diffused and enacted through *receptor sites* in individual countries (Frank, Hironaka and Schofer 2000).

With the case of the rise of animal protection, governmental ministries are used to diffuse and enforce elements of world-level culture, including the concept of animal protection as a definitive characteristic of the ideal and progressive nation-state. As a consequence of the expansion of world-level cultural expectations regarding the role of nation-states, most notably in the twentieth century, animal protection has become increasingly institutionalized and codified in law. An important puzzle for the future construction of world-level cultural values emerges from the convergence of animal protection and of increased meat consumption, with animal protection itself being redefined in terms of individual rights and increased meat consumption eventually, perhaps even soon, becoming an ecological impossibility.

Chapter Five

Animal Protection and Non-Governmental Organizations

As the twenty-first century begins, animal protection clearly has become the responsibility of the state. Although not having the political power of nation-states and other governmental entities, non-governmental organizations have contributed to the world-wide rise of animal protection. Much more so than nation-states and other governmental organizations and institutions, NGOs have an extremely wide range of organizational forms, strategies, missions, and purposes. Additionally, NGOs are able to select and shape elements of culture strategically in ways that transcend statist boundaries, not only resonating with citizens at large in civil society, but directly influencing legislation at world, national, regional, and local levels. In particular, international NGOs use elements of world-level culture, itself interlaced with the ideology of progress, to direct political and social action along the channels shaped and supported by world-level culture.

In this chapter, the role of NGOs in the advancement of animal protection is examined, including how culture is used to define animal protection as a necessary characteristic of societies and their governments, as well as to direct individual and corporate actions related to animal protection. Different perspectives and definitions of NGOs and their influence and roles in civil society are presented, with the intent being to identify and understand how NGOs have contributed to the rise of animal protection as a valued cultural norm throughout the world. Similarly, the general purposes, goals, and activities of NGOs are discussed, with the intent being to better understand the particulars of those NGOs dedicated to animal protection.

The chapter includes a discussion of organizational, purposive, and rhetorical distinctions among NGOs dedicated to animal protection, as well as the values and goals held in common. Overall, animal protection, as a concept

58

and activity, is seen to be an element of world-level culture that is mediated and distributed through NGOs, with international NGOs being primary nodes in a nexus that includes regional, national, local, and topical NGOs.

DEFINING NGOS

Non-governmental organizations are private organizations that are not established by a government or by inter-governmental agreement. NGOs have the ability to participate in international affairs through their activities, and members usually have independent voting rights. NGOs include those identified as national or international, with a national NGO being involved with issues within a particular state, and an international NGO contending with issues across borders (Bernhardt and Macalister-Smith 2002). Additionally, all religious organizations, such as the Roman Catholic Church, Buddhist Peace Fellowship, and Labor Zionist Alliance are considered NGOs, with some pursuing regular NGO representation at the United Nations and other international venues. Historians have noted the growth in both number and importance of NGOS during the nineteenth century, and their subsequent expansion of stature and influence (Charnovitz 1996).

Examples of national NGOs include an extremely varied range of organizations, such as the National Rifle Association, a United States organization that focuses on Second Amendment Rights and promotion of firearm-related activities (Rodengen and Maysonet 2002), the Namibia Nature Foundation, which promotes sustainable development, bio-diversity, and conservation of resources in Namibia (Brown, Tarr and Storm 2002), and the Lotus Children's Centre, which fills basic needs of children and impoverished families in Mongolia (Mongolian Foundation for Open Society 2003). International NGOs, also extremely varied, include global organizations such Amnesty International, which works for internationally recognized human rights and the impartial protection of those rights (Power 2001), Médecins Sans Frontières, an international medical humanitarian organization that delivers emergency aid to people affected by armed conflict, epidemics and natural and man-made disasters (Bortolotti 2004), and Greenpeace, an international organization that focuses on worldwide threats to global biodiversity and environment (Weyler 2004). NGOs can be focused on issues in specific regions, such as FACE, a European organization dedicated to promoting hunting, biodiversity, conservation, and preservation of wildlife habitats (Federation of Associations for Hunting and Conservation of the European Union 2003), and Avalon, a foundation that supports sustainable rural development based on organic agriculture in Central and Eastern Europe (Avalon 2005).

The purposes, goals and activities of NGOs are as widely ranging and diversified as human experience itself. NGOs may have a purely educational purpose, such as the Federation of Galaxy Explorers' mission to prepare children for the challenge of space exploration and Gluya's distribution of texts from Torah-observant organizations. Chicos Perdidos, concerned with issues involving missing children in Argentina, including prostitution and organ trafficking, is an example of organizations that practice direct action aimed at urgent and immediate threats. Since its formation after WWII, the United Nations has defined NGOs simply as "non-governmental organizations" that are part of the international community (Fassbender 1998; Simma et al. 2002; United Nations 2002). In 1968, Resolution 1296 of the Economic and Social Council of the United Nations defined and limited involvement of NGOs to consultative status, arguably exerting a type of control on how NGOs structured themselves, but still simply defining them as organizations that are not states (Otto 1996). Although historically there have been tensions between state actors and non-governmental actors, and disagreement over the extent to which NGOs should be allowed to participate, the trend recently has been to invite increased NGO involvement in all UN activities (United Nations 1996).

The influence of NGOs is perhaps better understood in the broader context of civil society. Alexis de Tocqueville understood civil society to be free associations existing as intermediate institutions through which citizens realize their social freedom and equality (Woldring 1998). Grounded in a theoretical tradition that embraces de Tocqueville's pluralist approach, Cohen and Arato assert that modern civil society is based on egalitarian principles and universal inclusion, and that citizens' active participation is crucial to the reproduction of democracy. They further argue for a conception of civil society that not only reflect modernity's "core of new collective identities," but also sets the terms by which these collectives can contribute to the "emergence of freer, more democratic" societies. Civil society in this model emerges from a cultural-linguistic background as "the institutional framework of a modern lifeworld stabilized by fundamental rights that include within their scope both the private and the public spheres" (1992). In other words, civil society thus conceptualized is grounded in a cultural-linguistic sub-stratum and encourages the emergence and development of horizontal networks. Both the universally held ability to communicate and horizontal networks are seen as countering the destructive properties of the increasingly rationalized lifeworld and corporately dominated market systems suggested in the work of Habermas (1987).

The influence of culture on active political participation can occur at several levels and in different ways. A societal definition of "good citizen" may be constructed using elements from a set of cultural elements held in common, such as the narrative "a good citizen is one who fights for justice and freedom." At the group or community level, however, the interpretation of that same definition will vary according to the specific cultural bias, with terms such as *citizen, justice,* and *freedom* having several possible meanings, each with different consequences for political action. In this respect, culture can be seen as both providing unity at the institutional and organizational level as well as influencing strategies of transformative political action.

Civil society, also referred to as the third sector or non-profit sector, can be described as an "area of association and action independent of the state and the market in which citizens can organize to pursue purposes that are important to them, individually and collectively" (Brown et al. 2000). Asserting that NGOs are manifestations of civil society interests, Teegan, Doh, and Vachani define NGOs as "private, not-for-profit organizations that aim to serve particular social interests by focusing advocacy and/or operational efforts on social, political and economic goals, including equity, health, education, health, environmental protection and human rights" (2004). NGOs, as manifestations of civil society, can be seen as engines of social transformation, not only providing a medium for advocacy (Keck and Sikkink 1998), but serving to provide resources and services that address pressing social conditions (Henderson 2002)

The influence of NGOs has increased sharply since the 1970s, and even though states are still considered the primary actors in world affairs, some have suggested that the steady accumulation of power by states, occurring since the Peace of Westphalia in 1648, is ending (Hartwick 2003; Mathews 1997). NGOs are influential for several reasons: they offer expertise and experience and often serve in an educational capacity (Leonard 2002); they bring attention to issues ignored by states (Anderson 2000; Bock and Human 2002); NGOs produce narratives that define citizenship and civil society (Smith 2004); and NGOs bring claims of victims before international commissions and tribunals (Cohen 1990; Olz 1997). Additionally, the important relationship between NGOs, social movements, and global change has been confirmed, documented, and analyzed (Colas 2002; Eschle and Stammers 2004; Moghadam 2000).

With an eye towards understanding NGOs, world-level culture, and animal protection, it is helpful to discuss existing theoretical approaches to the relationships between NGOs, social movements, and global change. One approach, presented in the work of Eschle and Stammers, is that existing theories and scholarship can be grouped into categories of *pragmatic, structuralist,* and *transformationalist* (2004). Pragmatists are grounded both in a social-democratic ideology that has a normative interest in the success of

the movements they study and in an empiricist epistemology, often empha-
sizing formal organization and assuming that the basis of political life is the
interface between state and non-state organizations (Riddell-Dixon 1995;
Tarrow 1998; Willets 2001). Structuralist approaches often draw on Marxist
or poststructuralist arguments and assume that all elements of movements are
shaped or even determined by deep social structure, processes, and institutions. Movements and NGOs are understood in terms of structural changes in
capitalism and the appropriation of movements by capitalist and state institutions, with substantially less attention, if any, to movement activism, organization, or strategy (Arrighi, Hopkins and Wallerstein 1989; Cox 1994; Gorg
and Hirsch 1998). Transformationalists, sometimes perceived as utopian,
present social movements and their organizations as having great emancipa-
tory potential, as well as having similar organizational structures and goals
(Castells 1997; Falk 1987; Otto 1996).

The distinctions made between NGOs, international NGOs, transnational
social movement organizations, and social movements all vary depending on
the ideological position and theoretical approach of theorists and scholars.
Whether they are claiming intellectual objectivity or self-identifying as activists, experts from various perspectives and disciplines agree that NGOs are
expanding their influence, and that INGOs are playing increasingly important
roles on the world stage.

NGOs contribute to social change by generating public interest in issues,
mobilizing resources, and addressing issues ignored or marginalized by
states, international, and supranational institutions. Capturing the attention
and material resources of both the public and state entities involves successful use of elements of culture, including ideas, images, and language.

Regarding the transformation of deeply embedded patterns of social behavior and meaning, in particular how humans mediate their relationship with
animals used for food and the enforcement of humane treatment, NGOs nec-
essarily appeal to a shared reservoir of cultural meaning relatively au-
tonomous, or at least distinguishable, from the social, political, or economic
spheres.

CULTURE AND NGOS

Social change or transformation is the restructuring of interpersonal, inter-
group, and institutional relationships, all involving individuals who share cultural understandings. The ability to engage in political action, including institutional reform, arguably increases where there are shared experiences,
memories, meanings, and motives. Culture can be seen as a resource, in that

it is acquired, shared, and used to fulfill the needs, wants, or desires of a group. This resource can be used to shape, initiate, and guide political action that engages, critiques, or defines the organization and distribution of power in society. Culture can be understood as experience, both the mundane and the ineffable, codified in such a way that others may understand or recognize that same experience as something meaningful outside of its original space and time. People recognize shared meanings and intentions through commonly held images, symbols, or narratives, and it is this recognition that provides context for collective political action at the organizational and institutional levels.

Culture in general can be described as the reservoir of language, symbols, ideas, and material artifacts available to members of a particular social system. Although there have been debates regarding the causal role of culture, there is consensus regarding the material and non-material aspects of culture, with the former referring to objects that are made or transformed by a members of a social system, and the latter including language, symbols, and ideas. Likewise, most approaches agree that culture is perceived by the members of a social system as having an authority that transcends personal choice and individual behavior. As to the theoretical debates surrounding the role of culture, the discourse on causality has for the most part set aside the cultural determinism associated with functionalism, and moved toward analyses of culture informed both by innovation in the field of sociology and by theoretical work from other disciplines.

Analyses that emphasize culture as a resource, rather than the provider of values that direct actions, are contributing to a deeper understanding of human individual and collective action. Proposing an alternative to the traditional model of culture, Ann Swidler formulates an analysis of culture that identifies and examines the formal elements, effects, and causal significance of culture, and how it influences action. Swidler identifies the formal elements of culture as symbols, stories, rituals, and world-views, all of which people use to solve problems, while the effects of culture are analyzed by identifying persistent "strategies of action." The causal significance of culture, according to Swidler, is to be found not in how it defines action, but rather in how members use its components, or formal elements, to construct "strategies of action" (1986).

Also viewing culture as a resource, Pierre Bourdieu conceptualizes cultural resources as *cultural capital*, which he identifies as having three different states: dispositional, institutional, and objectified. In Bourdieu's model, culture overall is a form of knowledge that allows the possessor to understand or to interpret cultural relations and artifacts. It is an internalized code and a learned ability to associate certain meanings with certain symbolic forms or goods, that is distributed and reproduced through "familial strategies" and educational institutions (Bourdieu 1998). Learning the appropriate interpretations of symbolic forms and goods, be they language, artifact, or concepts, is part of socialization. Once learned, this dispositional element of cultural capital predisposes individuals towards the accepted meaning of symbolic goods (Bourdieu 1993). This dispositional state includes the specialized abilities to use cultural capital in its objectified form. Objectified cultural capital includes any objects, including artistic images, texts, and music, that have meaning and interest only for those individuals who possess the learned cultural competence to interpret the code imbedded in elements of the particular culture (Bourdieu 1984). Cultural capital, as a resource, is seen as contributing to all social relations of power (Bourdieu 1993).

Swidler refers to *strategies of action*, a term that implies a collective calculation of how to most effectively participate in social relations of power, At first glance, this use of the term *strategy* appears similar to Foucault's employment of the term found in his analysis of relations of power, which emphasizes "ends," gaining an "advantage," and obtaining "victory" (Foucault 1994). However, referring again to Geertz, Swidler defines strategy as a "way of organizing action" that would allow for the realization of several goals, rather than being a conscious plan directed at a particular goal (Swidler 1986). One similarity can be found in Foucault's explanation that *strategy* is defined "by the choice of winning solutions," and involves individuals or collectives selectively engaging in strategies (Foucault 1994).

Drawing from both the interpretive model presented by Geertz and Swidler, and the critical analyses of Bourdieu and Foucault, culture can be understood as a resource that influences political action. The "repertoire," from which members construct "strategies of action" is developed, distributed, and reproduced through familial and institutional practices that are intermeshed with social relations of power. Although, as Swidler asserts, there may be no conscious use of culture to achieve a certain goal, culture is a resource that people use when strategically engaging in social relations of power, and as such may involve what Foucault describes repeatedly as "rationality functioning to arrive at an objective" (1994).

The role of international NGOs, often theorized using the concepts of civil society, international relations, and global governance, can also be understood in terms of cultural reproduction and social change. NGOs, whether conceptualized as normative political process or as transformative social movement organizations (TSMOs), involve the organization and mobilization of resources around a social issue or idea. Individuals and institutions respond to threats and risks, not simply in terms of economic or political power, but to ideas, concepts, symbols, and images framed and meditated by NGOs. This process takes place whether or not an NGO is formally linked, either organizationally or substantively, to a social movement.

As a medium of cultural reproduction, NGOs present, support, and disperse cultural norms, yet NGOs are also directly involved in social change in their roles as advocates and service providers. For example, Amnesty International supports and disperses norms of global civil society, specifically those related to human rights, yet is clearly an agent of social change, in both an educational role and an advocacy role. Although not a social movement, Amnesty International draws from a reservoir of cultural elements, and frames issues and events so that they convey specific meaning to state and individual actors that prompts a set of responses.

International NGOs are conveyers of culture and social change. Although sometimes affiliated with or having characteristics similar to social movements or TSMOs, INGOs are distinctive in that they exist through the voluntary actions of individuals, they have explicit, rationalized goals, they adhere to strong norms of open membership and democratic decision-making processes, and they attempt to spread progress throughout the world. Ideologically, INGOs are grounded in world-level cultural principles of universalism, individualism, rational voluntaristic authority, human purposes of rationalizing progress, and world citizenship (Boli and Thomas 1997). Although states have become the administrators and enforcers of the legal protection of animals, it is non-governmental actors that shape and change the ideas, attitudes, and values involved in human perception and institutional enactment of animal protection.

ANIMAL PROTECTION AND NGOS

The number of organizations dedicated to animal protection has grown from several dozen in the early nineteenth century to a current roster in the thousands (Guither 1998). World Animal Net, the world's largest network of animal protection societies with official consultative status at the United Nations, currently lists over 15,000 animal protection organizations in their global directory (World Animal Net 1999). As with NGOs in general, the role of these organizations involves education, advocacy, and coordination of resources and expertise. Many of these NGOs are staffed with self-identified activists, and claim affiliation with an international animal protection movement that can be described as a global epistemic community promoting animal protection as a primary characteristic, perhaps even a condition, of global citizenship.

Although not the only means of differentiation, animal protection NGOs can be categorized by focus, level of organization, and type of political engagement. There are federations of organizations that fall into a wide range of categories within animal protection, including animal management, animal rights, wildlife conservation, and biodiversity. The countries that have the longest history with industrialized meat economies tend to be home to groups addressing farm animals, as well as all other areas of animal protection and rights. Countries that have more recently modernized or have had minimal involvement in global meat economies tend to have some groups that protect wildlife, companion animals, or address biodiversity and sustainable development, but much less, if any, that address farm animals or animals used for food purposes. For the most part, animal protection NGOs emerged from existing political cultures in Europe and North America, and have been extended into other regions of the world as a consequence of a larger globalizing process.

Animal protection INGOs can be concerned with all animal issues or organized around specific groups of animals, such as marine mammals or farm animals. Membership is usually defined either in terms of individuals or organizations, but at both these levels, membership involves recognition of global norms of animal protection. The type of political engagement recommended and practiced by various INGOs ranges from passive contribution to radical activism, as well as from consumer education to legislative reform. World Animal Net (WAN) is a global network that accepts only organizations as affiliates, has no individual membership, is concerned with all aspects of animal protection, and has consultative status at the United Nations. WAN is a coalition for campaigning and political lobbying, with stated goals of focusing the animal protection movement and strengthening animal campaigns. Even though it has radical affiliates, WAN attempts to direct all organizational efforts into legislative reform (World Animal Net 1999).

Another federated INGO, Eurogroup for Animal Welfare (EAW), works to reduce animal suffering throughout Europe by promoting animal welfare as a core element of sustainable development, and focuses on European Union policy development and enforcement of European laws (Eurogroup for Animal Welfare 2004). Organizations that join EAW have missions and goals that echo those of EAW, and as affiliates have access to EAW institutional channels. While federations accept organizations as members (affiliates), the affiliates of federated groups typically have memberships comprised of individuals, such as Animalia Federation for the Protection of Animals. Animalia, supported by individual membership and an affiliate of EAW, is Finland's largest animal protection organization, and works for inclusion of animal welfare in morals and legislation through collaborative efforts with authorities (Animalia 2005).

Unlike federations such as Eurogroup for Animal Welfare and World Animal Net, Compassion in World Farming (CIWF) is an INGO comprised of individual members, with representatives in almost all regions of the world (Compassion in World Farming 2005). The rhetoric of CIWF is that of grassroots mobilization around global issues, such as the export of live animals, international transport of live animals, and reformation of the World Trade Organization's trade rules regarding animals (Pickett 2005). Like most INGOs, CIWF constructs participation in terms of global citizenship, with animal protection being a definitive characteristic of a humane and just society. Global animal issues are identified, presented, and explained to the public, with the recommended political action directed at the level of individual citizen, including letter writing, circulation of petitions, and consumer boycotts. Individual members are educated on certain issues and the importance of animal protection to global, regional, and local communities. Although the organization depends on grassroots participation at the individual level, the values and issues emanate from a world-level cultural reservoir created through global civil society.

INGOs not only disperse elements of world-level culture to individuals, they also reinforce its values and ideals. The Animal Welfare Institute (AWI), originally formed in response to the needs of animals used in experimentation, now directs much of its resources towards alleviating animal suffering globally in factory farms and in the fur trade (Animal Welfare Institute 2005a). Although AWI is supported by individual memberships and recommends standard grassroots participation, it shapes and reinforces an ideal of animal protection through the AWI Annual Albert Sweitzer Medal, awarded for outstanding achievement in the advancement of animal protection. Since its inception in 1951, the Sweitzer Medal has gone to high-profile individuals, from various countries, in politics, scientific research, law enforcement, and the media (Animal Welfare Institute 2005b). Although a few of the recipients can be described as radical activists, most work in formal organizations and have been recognized as exemplifying animal protection through their work in an institutional setting.

World-level cultural values and ideas are dispersed through international and national organizations and institutions. Social progress and humane action are defined at the institutional level, then taught or reproduced in the individual actor, who participates in the reinforcement and revision of world-level culture. Education has been a primary instrument of change regarding perceptions of non-human animals. Since mid-twentieth century, international organizations have funded, organized, and maintained animal-related educational projects wherever standardized educational institutions have appeared. These educational projects, whether they be grassroots mobilization around global animal issues, researching and presenting reports on state policy, or socialization of children, all involve dispersal and reinforcement of concepts and ideas that define the type of human-animal relationship expected of citizens. The diversity of approaches, both presently and in the past, to this relationship attests to the significance of culture, as seen in human interaction with one of the world's most numerous species, *bos taurus* (cow). The cow is worshipped in regions of India, but unceremoniously slaughtered and eaten in other regions of the world. Cows are the objects of bloodsport in Spain, but as rescued victims of factory farming, live comfortable lives on sanctuary lands in New York. As a icon, the ubiquitous cow is both a symbol of idyllic rural domesticity and of chaotic pandemic disease.

As with other assumptions in world-level culture, such as the necessity of the state for social order and of mass education for national development (Boli and Thomas 1997), humane treatment of animals has emerged as principle of world-level culture. Although states administrate and enforce codified principles of animal protection, non-governmental organizations have come to play an increasingly important role in the construction of animal protection as a characteristic of a modern state, as well as valued trait in the individual. The World Society for the Protection of Animals (WSPA), for example, works to ensure that the principles of animal welfare are universally understood and respected and protected by enforced legislation and to raise the standards of animal welfare throughout the world (World Society for Protection of Animals 2005). WSPA implements this through campaigns, rescue programs, and educational programs that define animal protection from a global perspective, and encourage local, regional, and national adoption of this perspective. WSPA sponsored Kindness Clubs for children in South America in the early 1970s, then later in Africa, and most recently in Indonesia, with the intention being that of teaching children to understand environmental protection, respect for all forms of life, and the needs of animals, including the domesticated animals most familiar to these children. Similarly, WSPA designed and promoted a "Concepts in Animal Welfare" syllabus and supportive network in 2000 that has been integrated into veterinary schools in diverse regions throughout the world.

Animal protection is seen not only as a characteristic value of a humane society, but as contributing to the formation of individual members. This value is an element of world-level culture, as exemplified in the rhetoric of a specialist in childhood education: "as future leaders, teachers, policymakers, and conscientious citizens, children can utilize their training and the spirit of animal advocacy to make this world a better place for all beings" (Pattnaik 2004:99). NGOs are instrumental in the institutionalization of animal protection, whether it be through direct action regarding legislation, in the promotion of certain values in adults, or in the early socialization of children. Legislation, at the international, national, regional, and local levels, is shaped by the pressures and resources of NGOs. Awards given to individuals or corporate entities reinforce animal protection as a characteristic of the ideal global citizen and as a value of world-level culture in general. Through the efforts of NGOs globally, early socialization of children includes learning world-level culture values grounded in an ideology of progress, as well as specific values supportive of animal protection. At all of these levels and in all of these activities, animal protection, as a value and goal of world-level culture, is mediated and distributed through NGOs, with international NGOs being primary nodes in a nexus that includes regionally, nationally, and locally based NGOs.

Conclusion

The Rise of Protection and Decline of Consumption

During the twentieth century, rapid changes occurred in human perceptions of the value and status of non-human animals. Institutional and individual concern for animal protection increased, as did global levels of meat consumption, most notably in developed, core countries.

These concurrent shifts, in the status of non-human animals and in levels of global meat consumption, were both grounded in an ideology of progress that promotes both animal protection and improved nutrition for all citizens. This ideology of progress is a fundamental element of world-level culture, and is conveyed through a nexus that includes nation-states and NGOs. Animal protection is both a value and a goal of world-level culture, with the ideal society and citizen expected to manifest these values and goals. The convergence of animal protection and increased meat consumption, both promoted as characteristics of the *progressive* or *improved* society, now presents the construction of world-level culture with the problem of its own conflicting values and goals.

ANIMAL PROTECTION AS
A CHARACTERISTIC OF PROGRESS

In the eighteenth century, European philosophers and scientists challenged existing dominant ideas, primarily promulgated through religious culture, regarding the status of non-human animals. As the authority of religious institutions waned, it was replaced in part by the authority of reason and science. Epistemic communities began to redefine existing understandings of political power, dominance, rights, and community, with the status and treatment of

71

non-human animals beings an explicitly stated concern. The ideology emerging from these eighteenth and nineteenth century epistemic communities defined progress as a consequence of rational inquiry and critique, and of necessity involving equality, justice, benevolence, and the concern for alleviation of suffering in its individual and collective forms.

During the nineteenth century, citizens increasingly viewed animals as creatures that could feel and suffer, and therefore should be protected under the mandate of the progressive society. These views were further supported and developed by scientists and philosophers in nineteenth century epistemic communities, dispersed through a nexus of association, and enacted by writers, political leaders, and other influential citizens.

By the end of the nineteenth century, animal protection was seen as a definitive characteristic of the modern, progressive society. Humane treatment of animals, involving explicit acknowledgement of their ability to suffer and feel pain, was believed to be directly related to both the reduction of violence and the increase of benevolence in society. Urban elites, aristocrats, philanthropists, educators, and the secularized descendants of religious reformers used their social and political status to promote animal protection as a necessary value and goal of both the ideal citizen and the ideal society. Animal protection had become a definitive characteristic of the ideal, progressive society.

MEAT CONSUMPTION AS
A CHARACTERISTIC OF PROGRESS

Another characteristic of the ideal, progressive society was the elimination of all forms of inequality. By the early nineteenth century, a meatless diet was increasingly viewed as a preventable form of economic and nutritional deprivation. Social activists, members of the scientific and medical communities, and political leaders all framed the meatless diet as yet another way in which the working class and poor were exploited. This exploitation was viewed as evidence of inequality between citizens, and thus a barrier to overall progress in society.

Early in the nineteenth century, hospitals, prisons, and municipalities began practicing the ideas, philosophies, and theories, all grounded in an ideology of progress, that supported the democratization of meat consumption. During the late nineteenth century, the modernization of meat production, including refrigeration, canning, railways, factory farming, and industrial slaughterhouses, responded and contributed to the increasing rate of meat consumption.

By the twentieth century, meat consumption was being further developed as an ideological component of progress. Theories and practices of modernization, economic development, and related public health, all grounded in a shared ideology of progress, contributed to meat consumption becoming a sharply increasing, global phenomenon throughout the twentieth century. As with animal protection, meat consumption had become a definitive characteristic of the ideal, progressive society.

ANIMAL PROTECTION AND WORLD CULTURE

The increase in animal protection legislation reflects the global expansion of a world-level culture that asserts the protection of animals as a primary value and goal of nation-states and their citizens. Global definitions of the nation-state during the twentieth century include animal protection as a characteristic of the ideal society, with nation-states adhering to the ideology of progress and accepting implementation of animal protection as evidence both of advancement and of global status. Nation-states and their ministries are used to diffuse and enforce elements of world-level culture, including animal protection as a value and a goal. As a consequence of the expansion of world-level cultural expectations, animal protection has become increasingly institutionalized through national and international legislation.

Non-governmental organizations have played crucial roles in the construction of animal protection as a characteristic of both the progressive state and its citizens. Whether through direct action regarding legislation, in promoting certain values in adults, or in the early socialization of children, NGOs have been instrumental in the global institutionalization of animal protection. Throughout the twentieth century, NGOs have funded, organized, and maintained animal-related educational projects, all of which involve the definition, dispersal, and reinforcement of the human-animal relationship expected of nation-states and citizens. Animal protection, as a value and goal of world-level culture, is mediated and distributed through NGOs at the global, national, regional, local, and individual levels, with international NGOs being primary nodes in a nexus that includes nationally, and locally based NGOs, as well as various governmental agencies of nation-states.

As the twenty-first century begins, world-level culture continues to be grounded in an ideology of progress that promotes both animal protection and the consumption of meat. Due to impending ecological constraints, one problem ahead lies in unraveling the convergence of two conflicting values of world-level culture. Animal protection is clearly a value and goal promoted by NGOs and legislated and enforced by nation-states, with both being in a nexus charged with the dispersal of elements of world culture. Similarly, consumption of meat continues to be ideologically framed as a necessary component of human nutrition, and thus a definitive characteristic of the progressive society. The current and future construction of world-level culture must include redefinition of this relationship between humans and other animals. Clearly, this redefinition has already begun, as evidenced by changes in the everyday lifeworld of citizens, ranging from the dramatic increase in consumption of meat-substitutes to the increased symbolic presentation, through various cultural mediums, of the inherent value of animals.

Of most pressing ecological concern is the human-animal relationship that involves the overwhelmingly most populated category of animals: that of animals raised, slaughtered, and protected as food for humans. The emergent norms that address this concern will be continue to be redefined at the world-cultural level, dispersed through channels in the nexus constructed and maintained by NGOs and governmental agencies, and finally internalized by individuals. Given our finite natural resources and our exponential population growth, the perceived necessity of meat consumption as an indicator of progress, wealth, and health will begin to recede, while the organized protection of animals will become an increasing priority, globally, of both corporate and individual actors.

References

Abel, Wilhelm. 1972. *Massenarmut und hungerkrisen im vorindustriellen Deutsch-land*. Göttingen: Vandenhoeck & Ruprecht.

———. 1986. *Agricultural fluctuations in Europe: From the thirteenth to the twenti-eth centuries*. London: Methuen.

Adams, Carol. 1993. Feeding on Grace: Institutional Violence, Christianity, and Veg-etarianism. In *Good news for animals?: Christian approaches to animal well-being*, edited by Jay B. McDaniel, 141–161. Maryknoll, NY: Orbis Books.

Adamson, Melitta Weiss. 2004. *Food in medieval times*. Westport, CT: Greenwood Press.

Ages, Arnold. 1999. The esthetics of style in Rousseau's epistolary polemics and the case of David Hume. *Neohelicon* 26:155–176.

American Humane Association. 1920. Report of the proceedings of the Annual Con-vention of the American Humane Association. River Falls, MA: American Humane Association.

American Society for the Prevention of Cruelty to Animals. 1866. *Objects, laws, etc., relating to the American Society for the Prevention of Cruelty to Animals*. New York: ASPCA.

———. 1905. Emily Appleton. *Our Animal Friends: An llustrated Monthly Magazine*, August.

Anderson, K. 2000. The Ottawa Convention Banning Landmines, the role of interna-tional non-governmental organizations and the idea of international civil society. *European Journal of International Law* 11:91.

Angell, George T. 1870. Jewish method of slaughtering. *Our Dumb Animals*, No-vember.

———. 1872. *Cattle transportation in the United States. An essay*. Boston: Massa-chusetts Society for the Prevention of Cruelty to Animals.

———. 1884. *Autobiographical sketches and personal recollections*. Boston: Franklin Press.

Animalia. 2005. *Animalia: Federation for the Protection of Animals*. Helsinki: Animalia.

Arrighi, Giovanni, Terence K. Hopkins, and Immanuel Maurice Wallerstein. 1989. *Antisystemic movements*. New York: Verso.

Asoka, King of Magadha. [259 BC]1958 *Edicts*. Chicago: University of Chicago Press.

Avalon. 2005. *Avalon: Opportunities and benefits offered by agri-environment schemes*. Wommels: Avalon.

Animal Welfare Institute. 2005a. *Animal Welfare Institute: History*. Washington, DC: AWI.

———. 2005b. *Animal Welfare Institute: The Sweitzer Medalists*. Washington, DC: AWI.

Balsys, Bodo. 2004. *Ahimsa: Buddhism and the vegetarian ideal*. New Delhi: Munshiram Manoharlal Publishers.

Barling, David, Tim Lang, and Martin Caraher. 2002. Joined-up food policy? The trials of governance, public policy and the food system. *Social Policy and Administration* 36:556–574.

Barrett, Julia R. 2001. Livestock farming: Eating up the environment? *Environmental Health Perspectives* 109:A312–A317.

Bartrip, Peter. 1985. Food for the body and food for the mind: The regulation of freshwater fisheries in the 1870s." *Victorian Studies* 28:285–304.

Bentham, Jeremy. [1789]1907. *An introduction to the principles of morals and legislation*. Oxford: Clarendon Press.

Bentham, Jeremy, J. H. Burns, and H. L. A. Hart. 1996. *An introduction to the principles of morals and legislation*. Oxford: Clarendon Press.

Berger, Peter L., and Thomas Luckmann. 1966. *The social construction of reality: A treatise in the sociology of knowledge*. Garden City, NY: Doubleday.

Berlin. 1871–1919. *Statistisches jahrbuch der Stadt Berlin*, in Jahrg. 1873/74 and Jahrg. 1915/19. Berlin: L. Simion.

Bernard, Leon. 1970. *The emerging city: Paris in the age of Louis XIV*. Durham, NC: Duke University Press.

Bernhardt, Rudolf, and Peter Macalister-Smith. 2002. *Encyclopedia of public international law*. Oxford: North-Holland.

Black, M.M. 2003. Micronutrient deficiencies and cognitive functioning. *Journal of Nutrition* 133:3927S-3931S.

Bock, Jane, and Katy Human. 2002. NGOs and the protection of biodiversity: The ecologists' views. *Colorado Journal of International Environmental Law and Policy* 13:168–181.

Boli, John, and George M. Thomas. 1997. World culture in the world polity: A century of international non-governmental organization. *American Sociological Review* 62:171–90.

Bonser, Kenneth J. 1970. *The drovers: Who they were and how they went: An epic of the English countryside*. London: Macmillan.

Booth, Charles. [1899]1970. *Life and labour of the people in London. Second series: Industry*. New York: AMS Press.

Bortolotti, Dan. 2004. *Hope in hell: Inside the world of Doctors Without Borders*. Buffalo, NY: Richmond Hill.

Bourdieu, Pierre. 1984. *Distinction: A social critique of the judgment of taste*. Cambridge.: Harvard University Press, 1984.

——. 1993. *The field of cultural production*. New York: Columbia University Press.

——. 1998. *Practical reason: On theory of action*. Stanford: Stanford University Press.

Bourdieu, Pierre, and Jean Claude Passeron. 1977. *Reproduction in education, society and culture*. Beverly Hills: Sage Publications.

Bourdieu, Pierre, and John B. Thompson. 1991. *Language and symbolic power*. Cambridge: Harvard University Press.

Bowditch, Henry I. 1868. Hippophagy. *New York Medical Journal* 7:386–413.

Boyd, William. 2001. Making meat: Science, technology, and American poultry production. *Technology and Culture* 42:631–664.

Brantz, Dorothee. 2002. Stunning bodies: Animal slaughter, Judaism, and the meaning of humanity in Imperial Germany. *Central European History* 35:167–194.

British Veterinary Association. 2004. Modernising animal welfare legislation: DEFRA launches its draft bill. *The Veterinary Record: Journal of the British Veterinary Association*, April.

Brown, Antony. 1974. *Who cares for animals?* London: Heinemann.

Brown, C. J., Jacquie Tarr, and Judy Storm. 2002. *Sustainable development in Namibia: Notes on environmental issues contributing toward sustainable development in Namibia*. Windhoek, NA: Ministry of Environment and Tourism.

Brown, L.D., S. Khagram, M.H. Moore, and P. Franklin. 2000. Globalization, NGOs, and multisectoral relations. In *Governance in a Globalizing World*, edited by Joseph S. Nye and John D. Donahue, 162–187. Washington, DC: Brookings Institution Press.

Bryant, Carol A. 2003. *The cultural feast: An introduction to food and society*. Belmont, CA: Wadsworth.

Buel, Clarence Clough. 1879. Henry Bergh and his work. *Scribner's*, April.

Buffon, Georges Louis Leclerc, comte de and William Smellie, trans. [1749]2000. *Natural history, general and particular*. Bristol: Thoemmes Press.

Bukkyo Dendo Kyokai. 1978. *The teaching of Buddha*. Tokyo: Bukkyo Dendo Kyokai.

Buxton, Thomas Fowell Sir. 1818. *An inquiry, whether crime and misery are produced or prevented, by our present system of prison discipline illustrated by descriptions of the borough Compter*. London: Butterworth and Son and J. Hatchard.

——. 1968[1839]. *The African slave trade and its remedy*. London: Dawsons.

——. 1984. *The papers of Sir Thomas Fowell Buxton, 1786–1845*. Brighton, ENG: Harvester Microform Publications.

Campbell, John L. 2002. Ideas, politics, and public policy. *Annual Review of Sociology* 28:21–38.

Carson, Gerald. 2003. Henry Bergh and the founding of the ASPCA. In *The animal rights movement*, edited by Kelly Wand, 64–71. San Diego: Greenhaven Press, 2003.

Castells, Manuel. 1997. *The power of identity*. Malden, MA: Blackwell.

Charnovitz, Steve. 1997. Two centuries of participation: NGOs and international governance. *Michigan Journal of International Law* 18:183–286.

Child, Lydia Maria Francis. [1865]1968. *The Freedmen's book*. New York: Arno Press.

Chirot, D., and T. D. Hall. 1982. World-system theory. *Annual Review of Sociology* 8:81–106.

Clark, Brett, and John Bellamy Foster. 2000. Henry S. Salt, socialist animal rights activist: An introduction to Salt's "A lover of animals." *Organization and Environment* 13:468–473.

Cobbett, William. [1853]2001. *Rural rides*. London: Penguin Books.

Cohen, Cynthia Price. 1990. The role of nongovernmental organizations in the drafting of the Convention on the Rights of the Child. *Human Rights Quarterly* 12:137–149.

Cohen, Jean L., and Andrew Arato. 1992. *Civil society and political theory*. Cambridge, MA: MIT Press.

Colas, Alejandro. 2002. *International civil society: Social movements in world politics*. Cambridge: Polity Press.

Coleman, James S. 1993. The rational reconstruction of society. *American Sociological Review* 58:1–15.

Compassion in World Farming. 2005. *Compassion in World Farming: Campaigning for farm animals*. Petersfield, ENG: CIWF.

Comte, Auguste, and Harriet Martineau. [1853]2001. *The positive philosophy of Auguste Comte*. Bristol: Thoemmes Press.

Cooper, John. 1993. *Eat and be satisfied: A social history of Jewish food*. Northvale, NJ: Jason Aronson.

Corsi, Pietro. 2005. Before Darwin: Transformist concepts in European natural history. *Journal of the History of Biology* 38:67–83.

Cox, Robert W. 1994. The crisis in world order and the challenge to international organization. *Cooperation and Conflict* 29:99–113.

Crawford, Michael A. 1992. The role of dietary fatty acids in biology: Their place in the evolution of the human brain. *Nutrition Reviews* 50:3–11.

Canadian Society for the Protection of Cruelty to Animals. 1873. *Canadian Society for the Prevention of Cruelty to Animals*. Montreal: Protestant Institution for Deaf-Mutes.

Darwin, Charles. 1874. *The descent of man, and selection in relation to sex*. New York: A.L. Burt.

——. [1871]1981. *The descent of man, and selection in relation to sex*. Princeton: Princeton University Press,.

——. [1871]1936. *The origin of species*. New York: Random House.

Davies, David. [1795]1977. *The case of labourers in husbandry stated and considered, with an appendix containing a collection of accounts shewing the earnings and expenses of labouring families in different parts of the kingdom*. Fairfield, NJ: A.M. Kelley.

Delgado, Christopher. 1997. The impact of livestock and fisheries on food availability and demand in 2020. *American Journal of Agricultural Economics* 79:1471–5.

Demment, Montague W., Michelle M. Young, and Ryan L. Sensenig. 2003. Providing micronutrients through food-based solutions: A key to human and national development. *Journal of Nutrition* 133:3879S-3885S.

Dennett, Daniel Clement. 1995. *Darwin's dangerous idea: Evolution and the meanings of life*. New York: Simon and Schuster.

Diderot, Denis. [1751]1977. *Melanges et morceaux divers: Contributions a l'histoire des deux Indes, tomo II*. Siena: Università di Siena.

Diderot, Denis, and Jean Le Rond Alembert. [1751]1965. *Encyclopedia*. Indianapolis: Bobbs-Merrill.

Dresner, Samuel H., Seymour Siegel, and David M. Pollock. 1982. *The Jewish dietary laws*. New York: Rabbinical Assembly of America United Synagogue Commission on Jewish Education.

Dyer, C. 1988. Changes in Diet in the Late Middle Ages: The Case of Harvest Workers. *Agricultural History Review* 36:21–37.

Eastman, Julia A. 1872. *Striking for the right*. Boston: D. Lothrop.

Edmonds, John W. 1868. *Statutes at large of the State of New York: Containing the general statutes passed in the years 1863, 1864, 1865 & 1866, with a reference to all the decisions upon them*. Albany, NY: Weed Parsons.

Empedocles, and M. R. Wright. 1995. *Empedocles: The extant fragments*. London: Classical Press.

Engels, Friedrich. [1845]1993. *The condition of the working class in England*. Oxford: Oxford University Press.

Eschle, Catherine, and Neil Stammers. 2004. Taking part: Social movements, INGOs, and global change. *Alternatives* 29:333–372.

Eurogroup for Animal Welfare. 2004. *Eurogroup for Animal Welfare annual report 2004*. Brussels: EAW.

Fabre-Vassas, Claudine. 1997. *The singular beast: Jews, Christians and the pig*. New York: Columbia University Press.

Fairholme, Edward G., and Wellesley Pain. 1924. *A century of work for animals: The history of the R.S.P.C.A., 1924–1924*. London: J. Murray.

Falk, Richard. 1987. The global promise of social movements: Explorations at the edge of time. *Alternatives* 12:173–196.

Farrell, Stephen. 2004. Commons sense: Richard Martin 'Humanity Dick' (1754–1834). *History Today* 54:60.

Fassbender, B. 1998. The United Nations Charter as constitution of the international community. *The Columbia Journal of Transnational Law* 36:529–619.

Federation of Associations for Hunting and Conservation of the European Union. 2003. *FACE manifesto*. Brussels: Federation of Associations for Hunting and Conservation of the EU.

Fenton, Alexander, and Eszter Kisban. 1986. *Food in change: Eating habits from the middle ages to the present day*. Atlantic Highlands, NJ: Edinburgh J. Donald Publishers and National Museums of Scotland.

Fitzmaurice, Edmond George Petty. 1895. *The life of Sir William Petty, 1623–1687 chiefly derived from private documents hitherto unpublished*. London: J. Murray.

Food and Agriculture Organization of the United Nations. 2005. FAOSTAT data. Rome: Food and Agriculture Organization of the UN.

Foucault, Michel. *Power*. 1994. New York: The New Press.

Francione, Gary L. 1996. *Rain without thunder: The ideology of the animal rights movement*. Philadelphia: Temple University Press.

———. 2000. *Introduction to animal rights: Your child or the dog?* Philadelphia: Temple University Press.

Frank, David John, Ann Hironaka, and Evan Schofer. 2000. The nation-state and the natural environment over the twentieth century. *American Sociological Review* 65:96–116.

Franklin, Adrian. 1999. *Animals and modern cultures: A sociology of human-animal relations in modernity*. London: Sage.

Gay, Peter. 1954. The Enlightenment in the history of political theory. *Political Science Quarterly* 69:374–389.

Gorg, Christoph, and Joachim Hirsch. 1998. Is international democracy possible? *Review of International Political Economy* 5:585–615.

Grant, Robert McQueen, ed. 1961. *Gnosticism: A source book of heretical writings from the early Christian period*. New York: Harper.

Grigg, D. 1993. The role of livestock products in world food-consumption. *Scottish Geographical Magazine* 109:66–74.

———. 1994. Income, industrialization and food-consumption. *Tijdschrift Voor Economische En Sociale Geografie* 85:3–14.

———. 1995a. The nutritional transition in western Europe. *Journal of Historical Geography* 21:247–261.

———. 1995b. The pattern of world protein consumption. *Geoforum* 26:1–17.

———. 1999. The changing geography of world food consumption in the second half of the twentieth century. *Geographical Journal* 165:1–11.

———. 2001. Food imports, food exports and their role in national food consumption. *Geography* 86:171–176.

Guinzburg, Rabbi. 1870. The Jewish Method of Slaughtering. *Our Dumb Animals*, December.

Guither, Harold D. 1998. *Animal rights: History and scope of a radical social movement*. Carbondale: Southern Illinois University Press.

Haas, Peter M. 1992. Introduction: Epistemic communities and international policy coordination. *International Organization* 4:1–36.

Habermas, Jurgen. 1987. *The theory of communicative action. vol.2, lifeworld and system: A critique of functionalist reason*. Cambridge: Polity.

Haenel, H. 1988. Comparison of nutrition habits in Potsdam two centuries ago with modern developments. *Nahrung* 32:153–179.

Hansen-Lappen, Karen. 1993. *Animals, people, and the MSPCA: 125 years of progress, 1868–1993*. Boston: Massachusetts Society for the Prevention of Cruelty to Animals.

Harlow, Alvin F. 1957. *Henry Bergh, founder of the A.S.P.C.A.* New York: J. Messner.

Harris, Marvin. 1965. The cultural ecology of India's sacred cattle. *Current Anthropology* 7:51–66.

Hartwell, R.M. 1961. The rising standard of living in England, 1800–1850. *Economic History Review* 13:402–427.

Hartwick, Jeffrey Andrew. 2003. Non-governmental organizations at United Nations-sponsored world conferences: A framework for participation reform. *Loyola of Los Angeles International and Comparative Law Review* 26:217–80.

Harvey, Barbara F. 1993. *Living and dying in England, 1100–1540: The monastic experience*. New York: Oxford University Press.

Henderson, Keith. 2002. Alternative service delivery in developing countries: NGOs and other non-profits in urban areas. *Public Organization Review* 2:99–116.

Hendrick, George. 1977. *Henry Salt, humanitarian reformer and man of letters*. Urbana: University of Illinois Press.

Herbert, Sandra. 2005. The Darwinian revolution revisited. *Journal of the History of Biology* 38:51–66.

Hesiod, David W. Tandy, and Walter C. Neale. 1996. *Hesiod's Works and Days*. Berkeley: University of California Press.

Hodgson, Geoffrey M. 1992. Marx, Engels and Economic Evolution. *International Journal of Social Economics* 19:121–130.

Hu, F.B. 2003. Plant-based foods and prevention of cardiovascular disease: An overview. *American Journal of Clinical Nutrition* 78:544S-551S.

Hughes, David. 1995. Animal welfare, the consumer and the food industry. *British Food Journal* 97:3–7.

Hull, David. 2005. Deconstructing Darwin: Evolutionary theory in context. *Journal of the History of Biology* 38:137–152.

Hulliung, Mark. 1994. *The autocritique of Enlightenment: Rousseau and the Philosophes*. Cambridge: Harvard University Press.

Hume, David. [1751]1998. *An enquiry concerning the principles of morals*. New York: Oxford University Press.

———. [1752]1963. Of the jealousy of trade. In *Essays: Moral, political and literary*. London: Oxford University Press.

Hussaini, Mohammad Mazhar. 1993. *Islamic dietary concepts and practices*. Bedford Park, IL: Islamic Food and Nutrition Council of America.

Iggers, Georg. 1965. The idea of progress: A critical assessment. *American Historical Review* 71:1–17.

Institute of Islamic Jurisprudence of UK. 1997. *Halaal Muslim food guide*. Batley: Al-Madina.

Johnson, Allen W., and Timothy K. Earle. 2000. *The evolution of human societies: From foraging group to agrarian state*. Stanford: Stanford University Press.

Johnston, Valerie J. 1985. *Diet in workhouses and prisons, 1835–1895*. New York: Garland.

Jones, Greta. 1980. *Social Darwinism and English thought: The interaction between biological and social theory*. Brighton, UK: Harvester Press.

Judd, Robin. 2003. The politics of beef: Animal advocacy and the kosher butchering debates in Germany. *Jewish Social Studies* 10:117–150.

Kalechofsky, Roberta. 1992. *Judaism and animal rights: Classical and contemporary responses*. Marblehead, MA: Micah Publications.

Kamminga, Harmke, and Andrew Cunningham. 1995. *The science and culture of nutrition, 1840–1940*. Amsterdam: Rodopi.

Kean, Hilda. 1998. *Animal rights: Political and social change in Britain since 1800*. London: Reaktion Books.

Keck, Margaret E., and Kathryn Sikkink. 1998. *Activists beyond borders: Advocacy networks in international politics*. Ithaca: Cornell University Press.

Knapp, Vincent J. 1997. The democratization of meat and protein in late eighteenth- and nineteenth-century Europe. *The Historian* 59:541–51.

Kook, Abraham Isaac. 1978. *Abraham Isaac Kook: The lights of penitence, the moral principles, lights of holiness, essays, letters, and poems*. New York: Paulist Press.

Kulling, Friedrich. 1977. *Bei uns wie uberall?: Antisemitismus*. Zürich: Schweizerischer Israelitischer Gemeindebund.

Laidlaw, James. 1995. *Riches and renunciation: religion, economy, and society among the Jains*. New York: Oxford University Press.

Lamarck, Jean Baptiste Pierre Antoine de Monet de. [1809]1984. *Zoological philosophy: An exposition with regard to the natural history of animals*. Chicago: University of Chicago Press.

Lane, Joan. 2001. *A social history of medicine: Health, healing and disease in England, 1750–1950*. New York: Routledge.

Lapidus, Ira M. 1988. *A history of Islamic societies*. Cambridge: Cambridge University Press.

Larsen, Clark Spencer. 2003. Animal source foods and human health during evolution. *Journal of Nutrition* 133:3893S-3897S.

Le Play, Frederic. 1982. *Frederic Le Play on family, work, and social change*. Chicago: University of Chicago Press.

Leach, Gerald. 1995. *Global land and food in the 21st century: Trends and issues for sustainability*. Stockholm: Stockholm Environment Institute

Leavitt, Emily Stewart, ed. 1990. *Animals and their legal rights: A survey of American laws from 1641 to 1990*. Washington, DC: Animal Welfare Institute.

Lenski, Gerhard Emmanuel, and Jean Lenski. 1987. *Human societies: An introduction to macrosociology*. New York: McGraw-Hill.

Leonard, Kenneth L. 2002. When both states and markets fail: Asymmetric information and the role of NGOs in African health care. *International Review of Law and Economics* 22:61–81.

Lewis, George H. 2000. From Minnesota fat to Seoul food: Spam in America and the Pacific Rim. *Journal of Popular Culture* 34:83–105.

Linne, Carl von. [1735]1964. *Systema naturae*. New York: Weinheim J. Kramer.

Linzey, Andrew. 1995. *Animal theology*. Urbana: University of Illinois Press.

Lupieri, Edmondo. 2002. *The Mandaeans: The last Gnostics*. Grand Rapids, MI.: W.B. Eerdmans.

Lynam, Shevawn. 1975. *Humanity Dick: A biography of Richard Martin, M. P., 1754–1834*. London: Hamilton.

Manu, and Ganganatha Jha. 1999. *Manusmrti: With the "Manubhasya" of Medhatithi*. Delhi: Marilal Banarsidass Publishers.

Masri, Al-Hafiz B. A. 1987. *Islamic Concern for Animals*. Petersfield, UK: Athene Trust.

Mathews, Jessica T. 1997. Are networks better than nations? *New Perspectives Quarterly* 14:10–13.

May, Trevor. 1995. *Gondolas and growlers: The history of the London horse cab*. Phoenix Mill: Alan Sutton.

McCrea, Roswell C. [1910]1969. *The humane movement: A descriptive survey prepared on the Henry Bergh Foundation for the Promotion of Humane Education in Columbia University.* College Park, MD: McGrath Pub. Co.

McGinn, Bernard, John Meyendorff, and Jean Leclercq. 1985. *Christian spirituality: Origins to the twelfth century.* New York: Crossroad.

Meyer, J. W. 1987. The world polity and the authority of the nation-state. In *Institutional structure: Constituting state, society, and the individual,* edited by George M. Thomas, J. W. Meyer, F. O. Ramirez, and J. Boli, 366–398. Newbury Park, CA: Sage.

Meyer, J. W., J. Boli, G. M. Thomas, and F. O. Ramirez. 1997. World society and the nation-state. *American Journal of Sociology* 103:144–181.

Meyer, John W., and Ronald L. Jepperson. 2000. The 'actors' of modern society: The cultural construction of social agency. *Sociological Theory* 18:100–120.

Milton, K. 2003. The critical role played by animal source foods in human (homo) evolution. *Journal of Nutrition* 133:3886S-3892S.

Moghadam, Valentine. 2000. Transnational feminist networks: Collective action in an era of globalization. *International Sociology* 15:57–85.

Mongolian Foundation for Open Society. 2003. *Directory of Mongolian NGOs.* Ulaanbaatar: MFOS.

Moss, Arthur W. 1961. *Valiant crusade: The history of the R.S.P.C.A..* London: Cassell.

Mottram, R. H. 1946. *Buxton the liberator.* London: Hutchinson and Co.

Massachusetts Society for the Prevention of Cruelty to Animals. 1868. Hippophagy. *Our Dumb Animals,* October.

———. 1873. Striking for the right. *Our Dumb Animals,* January.

———. 1874. Hippophagy. *Our Dumb Animals,* January.

Muhaiyaddeen, M. R. Bawa. 1985. *Come to the secret garden: Sufi tales of wisdom.* Philadelphia: Fellowship Press.

Murphy, S.P., and L.H. Allen. 2003. Nutritional importance of animal source foods. *Journal of Nutrition* 133:3932S-3935S.

New York Times. 1871. A friend of the friendless. June 5

———. 1875. Hippophagy. April 22.

Neild, William. 1841. Comparative statement of the income and expenditure of certain families of the working class in Manchester and Dukinfield, in the years 1836 and 1841. *Journal of the Statistical Society* 4:324–31.

Nisbet, Robert A. 1980. *History of the idea of progress.* New York: Basic Books.

Niven, Charles D. 1967. *History of the humane movement.* London: Johnson Publications.

Olz, Martin A. 1997. Non-governmental organizations in regional human rights systems. *Columbia Human Rights Law Review* 28:307–375.

Otto, Dianne. 1996. Nongovernmental organizations in the United Nations system: The emerging role of international civil society. *Human Rights Quarterly* 18:107–141.

Pattnaik, Jyotsna. 2005. On behalf of their animal friends: Involving children in animal advocacy. *Childhood Education* 81:95–101.

Paulus, Ingeborg. 1974. *The search for pure food: A sociology of legislation in Britain*. London: M. Robertson.

Pepys, Samuel. [1660–69]1970. *The diary of Samuel Pepys*. Berkeley: University of California Press.

Pereira, Jonathan. 1843. *A treatise on food and diet*. New York: Langley.

Perren, Richard. 1978. *The meat trade in Britain, 1840–1914*. London: Routledge and Kegan Paul.

Petty, William Sir. [1656]1997. *The history of the survey of Ireland: Commonly called the Down Survey*. London: Thoemmes Press.

Phelps, Norm. 2004. *The great compassion: Buddhism and animal rights*. New York: Lantern Books.

Pick, Philip L. 1977. *Tree of life: An anthology of articles appearing in the "Jewish Vegetarian," 1966–1974*. South Brunswick, NJ: A. S. Barnes.

Pickett, Heather. 2005. Stop the bull ship: The subsidized trade in live cattle from the European Union to the Middle East, annual report 2004. Petersfield, UK: Compassion in World Farming.

Pimentel, D., and M. Pimentel. 2003. Sustainability of meat-based and plant-based diets and the environment. *American Journal of Clinical Nutrition* 78:660S-663S.

Pollard, Sidney. 1959. *A history of labour in Sheffield*. Liverpool: Liverpool University Press.

Postel, Sandra. 1997. *Last oasis: Facing water scarcity*. New York: W.W. Norton.

Power, Jonathan. 2001. *Like water on stone: The story of Amnesty International*. Boston: Northeastern University Press.

Population Reference Bureau. 2004. *World population data, 2004*. Washington, DC: PRB.

Pullar, Philippa. 1970. *Consuming passions: A history of English food and appetite*. London: Hamilton.

Rachels, James. 1999. *Created from animals: The moral implications of Darwinism*. Oxford: Oxford University Press.

Radford, Mike. 2001. *Animal welfare law in Britain: Regulation and responsibility*. Oxford: Oxford University Press.

Regan, Tom. 1982. *All that dwell therein: Animal rights and environmental ethics*. Berkeley: University of California Press.

———. 1983. *The case for animal rights*. Berkeley: University of California Press.

———. 1990. Christianity and animal rights: The challenge and promise. In *Liberating life: Contemporary approaches to ecological theology*, edited by Jay B. McDaniel, 65–87. Maryknoll, NY: Orbis Books, 1990.

Richardson, N. J., H. MacFie, and R. Shepherd. 1994. Consumer attitudes to meat eating. *Meat Science* 36:57–66.

Riddell-Dixon, Elizabeth. 1995. Social movements and the United Nations. *International Social Science Journal* 47:289–305.

Riedweg, Christoph. 2005. *Pythagoras: His life, teaching, and influence*. Ithaca: Cornell University Press.

Rifkin, Jeremy. 1992. *Beyond beef: The rise and fall of the cattle culture*. New York: Dutton.

Rodengen, Jeffrey L., and Melody Maysonet. 2002. *NRA: An American legend*. Fort Lauderdale: Write Stuff Enterprises.

Rostow, W. W. 1960. *The stages of economic growth: A non-communist manifesto*. Cambridge, UK: Cambridge University Press.

Rousseau, Jean-Jacques. [1762]1997. *The social contract and other later political writings*. Cambridge, UK: Cambridge University Press.

Royal Society for the Prevention of Cruelty to Animals. 1872. Henry Bergh. *Animal World*, October 1.

———. 1888. The Late Henry Bergh. *Animal World*, April 2.

Rūmī, Jalal al-Din, and William C. Chittick. 1983. *The Sufi path of love: The spiritual teachings of Rumi*. Albany: State University of New York Press.

Sabate, J. 2003. The contribution of vegetarian diets to health and disease: A paradigm shift? *American Journal of Clinical Nutrition* 78:502S-507S.

Salt, Henry Stephens. 1894. *Animals' rights considered in relation to social progress: With a bibliographical appendix*. New York: Macmillan.

Sanghavarman, Jung-hsi Li. 1993. *The biographical scripture of King Asoka*. Berkeley: Numata Center for Buddhist Translation and Research.

Sarasua, Carmen. 2001. Upholding status: The diet of a noble family in early nineteenth-century La Mancha. In *Food, drink and identity: Cooking, eating and drinking in Europe since the middle ages*, edited by Peter Scholliers, 37–62. Oxford: Berg Publishers.

Scholliers, Peter, and C. Vandenbroeke. 1982. The transition from traditional to modern patterns of demand in Belgium. In *Consumer behaviour and economic growth in the modern economy*, edited by E. H. P. Baudet and Henk van der Meulen, 145–169. London: Croom Helm.

Schopenhauer, Arthur. [1841]1903. *The basis of morality*. London: G. Allen.

Scott, John, and R. Zaretsky. 2003. Rousseau and the revival of humanism in contemporary French political thought. *History of Political Thought* 24:599–623.

Scully, Matthew. 2002. *Dominion: The power of man, the suffering of animals, and the call to mercy*. New York: St. Martin's Press.

Sere, Carlos, Henning Steinfeld, and Jan Groenewold. 1996. *World livestock production systems: Current status, issues, and trends*. Rome: Food and Agriculture Organization of the UN.

Sewell, Anna. [1877]1990. *Black Beauty: The autobiography of a horse, translated from the original equine*. New York: Farrar Straus and Giroux.

Shimony, Abner. 1997. Some historical and philosophical reflections on science and enlightenment. *Philosophy of Science* 64:S1–S14.

Simma, Bruno, Hermann Mosler, Andreas Paulus, and Eleni Chaitidou. 2002. *The Charter of the United Nations: A commentary*. Oxford: Oxford University Press.

Singer, Peter. 1975. *Animal liberation: A new ethics for our treatment of animals*. New York: Random House.

Smith, Bruce D. 1998. *The emergence of agriculture*. New York: W.H. Freeman.

Smith, Edward. 1864. *Practical dietary for families, schools, and the labouring classes*. London: Walton and Maberly.

Smith, Margaret. 1978. *The way of the mystics*. Oxford: Oxford University Press.

———. 2001. *Muslim women mystics: The life and work of Rábià and other women mystics in Islam.* Oxford: Oneworld.

Smith, Matt. 2004. Mediating the world: Development, education and global citizenship. *Globalisation, Societies and Education* 2:1–24.

Sorabji, Richard. 1993. *Animal minds and human morals: The origins of the western debate.* Ithaca: Cornell University Press.

Speedy, A. W. 2003. Global production and consumption of animal source foods. *Journal of Nutrition* 133:4048S-4053S.

Spencer, Colin. 1996. *The heretic's feast: A history of vegetarianism.* Hanover, NH: University Press of New England.

Stark, William. 1788. *The works of the late William Stark, M.D.: Consisting of clinical and anatomical observations, with experiments, dietetical and statical.* London: J. Johnson.

Steele, Zulma. 1942. *Angel in top hat.* New York: Harper and Brothers.

Steinberg, Augusta, and Florence Guggenheim-Grünberg. 1966. *Geschichte der Juden in der Schweiz vom 16. jahrhundert bis nach der emanzipation.* Zürich: Schweizerischer Israelitischer Gemeindebund.

Stowe, Harriet Beecher. 1867. *Queer little people.* Boston: Ticknor and Fields.

Swidler, Ann. 1986. Culture in action: Symbols and strategies. *American Sociological Review* 51:273–286.

Tarrow, Sidney G. 1998. *Power in movement: Social movements and contentious politics.* Cambridge: Cambridge University Press.

Teegen, Hildy, Jonathan P. Doh, and Sushil Vachani. 2004. The importance of nongovernmental organizations (NGOs) in global governance and value creation: An international business research agenda. *Journal of International Business Studies* 35:463–483.

Teuteberg, H. J. 1971. Variations in meat consumption in Germany. *Ethnologia Scandinavica* 1:131–141.

———. 1975. European diet from pre-Industrial to modern times. In *Basic conditions of life,* edited by Elborg Forster and Robert Forster, 77–99. New York: Harper and Row.

Thomas, Keith. 1983. *Man and the natural world: A history of the modern sensibility.* New York: Pantheon Books.

United Nations. 1996. ECOSOC urges full NGO participation in UN. *UN Chronicle* 33:34.

———. 2001. *Report of the Secretary-General on agriculture, land and desertification.* New York: UN Commission on Sustainable Development.

———. 2002. *Charter of the United Nation; and, Statute of the International Court of Justice.* New York: UN Dept. of Public Information.

United States. 1956. *Humane slaughtering of livestock and poultry: hearings before a subcommittee of the Committee on Agriculture and Forestry, United States Senate, Eighty-fourth Congress, second session, on S. 1636, a bill to require the use of humane methods in the slaughter of livestock and poultry in interstate or foreign commerce, and for other purposes. May 9 and 10, 1956. Corp Author(s): United States. Congress. Senate. Committee on Agriculture, Nutrition, and Forestry. Subcommittee on S. 1636.* Washington, DC: United States Government.

United States Department of Agriculture. 1978. First federal law to prevent cruelty to animals. In *Animals and Their Legal Rights: A Survey of American Laws from 1641 to 1990*, edited by Emily Stewart Leavitt, 34–37. Washington, DC: Animal Welfare Institute.

———. 2004. *Agricultural Statistics, 2004*. Washington, DC: USDA.

Unti, Bernard Oreste. 2002. The quality of mercy: Organized animal protection in the United States, 1866–1930. PhD diss., American University.

Vedel, Jaques. 1975. La consommation Alimentaire dans le haut langaedol aux XVii et XVIII siecles. *Annales* 30:485–504.

Voice of Humanity. 1827. *The Voice of Humanity: Observations on a few of the instances of cruelty to animals, against which no legislative provision is made; abstracts of the present acts of Parliament available to the cause of humanity, with full remarks on their application; Hints on the formation and regulation of societies for the prevention of cruelty to animals*. London: Sherwood and Co.

Voltaire. [1740]1975. *Essai sur les moeurs et l'esprit des nations*. Paris: Editions Sociales.

Wallerstein, Immanuel Maurice. 1966. *Social change: The colonial situation*. New York: Wiley.

———. 1979. *The capitalist world-economy: Essays*. Cambridge: Cambridge University Press.

Walters, Kerry S., and Lisa Portmess. 1999. *Ethical vegetarianism from Pythagoras to Peter Singer*. New York: State University of New York Press.

———. 2001. *Religious vegetarianism: From Hesiod to the Dalai Lama*. Albany: State University of New York Press.

Watson, Adam. 1992. *The evolution of international society: A comparative historical analysis*. New York: Routledge.

Weitzman, Gideon, and Abraham Isaac Kook. 1999. *Sparks of light: Essays on the weekly Torah portions based on the philosophy of Rav Kook*. Northvale, NJ: Jason Aronson.

Weyler, Rex. 2004. *Greenpeace: How a group of journalists, ecologists and visionaries changed the world*. Emmaus, PA: Rodale.

Willets, Peter. 2001. Transnational actors and international organizations. In *The Globalization of World Politics: An Introduction to International Relations*, edited by John Baylis and Steve Smith, 238–272. New York: Oxford University Press.

Woldring, Henk E. S. 1998. State and civil society in the political philosophy of Alexis de Tocqueville. *Voluntas* 9:363–373.

Wood, Neal. 1992. Tabula rasa, social environmentalism, and the 'English Paradigm'. *Journal of the History of Ideas* 53:647–688.

World Animal Net. 1999. *World Animal Net directory: International directory of animal protection organisations*. Boston: World Animal Net.

World Society for the Protection of Animals. *WSPA: About us*. London: WSPA.

Young, James Harvey. 1989. *Pure food: Securing the "Federal food and drugs act of 1906."* Princeton: Princeton University Press.

Zemel, Babette, Phyllis B. Eveleth, and Francis E. Johnston. 1999. *Human growth in context*. London: Smith-Gordon.

Index

abolitionists, 46, 47, 48, 50
Africa, 32, 68
agrarian societies, 28–29, 36
agricultural workers, 30
Alinsky, Saul, 47
American Society for the Prevention of Cruelty to Animals (ASPCA), 20, 48–51
Angell, George, 47–48, 50–52
animal protection, historical emergence of, 1–3, 8–12, 13–26, 47
animal rights, 2, 8–10, 17–18, 41, 50, 66
Animal Welfare Institute (AWI), 56, 67
Appleton, Emily, 48, 50
Argentina, 32, *33–34*, 35, 60
aristocracy, 7, 40, 72
Australia, 10, 31–34, *33–34*

Belgium, 32
Benedictines, 29
Bentham, Jeremy, 16, 26, 43
Berger, Peter, 12
Bergh, Henry, 47–50, 52
Bogomils, prohibitions against eating meat, 42
Bourdieu, Pierre, 12, 63–64
Britain, 17, 27, 32, 43–44, 53
Buddhism, 14–16, 41

Buffon, Georges, 25–25
Bush, George, 56
Buxton, Thomas Fowell, 44

Canada, 10, 20, 53, 55
Canadian Society for the Protection of Animals (CSPA), 20
Caribbean, *33–34*
Cathars, prohibitions against eating meat, 42
cattle, 6–7, 19, 32, 43–44, 46–53
Christianity, 14–16, 29, 41, 43
citizenship, concept of, 5, 12, 20, 26, 38, 58–61, 65
civil society, 58–61, 64–67
colonization, 31–31
Compassion in World Farming (CIWF), 67
Comte, Auguste, 21, 25
cultural capital, 63–64
culture, 3, 7, 11–12, 36–37, 58, 60–66, 68

Darwin, Charles, 17–18, 24–25
Department for Environment, Food, and Rural Affairs (DEFRA), 54–55
developed countries, 2, 6–8, 31–53, *33–35*
Diderot, Denis, 21–22